GW01276026

The
Highland Division

Eric Linklater

MLRS
2004

Printed by JRDigital Print Services Ltd, Whitstable, KENT CT5 3PD

ORDER OF BATTLE

The Fifty-First (Highland) Division

MAJOR-GENERAL V. M. FORTUNE, C.B., D.S.O.

1ST BN. THE LOTHIANS & BORDER HORSE (YEOMANRY).

152ND BRIGADE: BRIGADIER H. W. V. STEWART, D.S.O.
2nd Bn. The Seaforth Highlanders.
4th Bn. The Seaforth Highlanders.
4th Bn. The Queen's Own Cameron Highlanders.

153RD BRIGADE: BRIGADIER G. T. BURNEY, M.C.
4th Bn. The Black Watch.
1st Bn. The Gordon Highlanders.
5th Bn. The Gordon Highlanders.

154TH BRIGADE: BRIGADIER A. C. L. STANLEY-CLARKE, D.S.O.
1st Bn. The Black Watch.
7th Bn. The Argyll & Sutherland Highlanders.
8th Bn. The Argyll & Sutherland Highlanders.

THE ROYAL ARTILLERY: C.R.A., BRIGADIER H. C. H. EDEN, M.C.
17th Field Regiment, Royal Artillery.
23rd Field Regiment, Royal Artillery.
75th Field Regiment, Royal Artillery.
51st Anti-tank Regiment, Royal Artillery.

THE ROYAL ENGINEERS: C.R.E., LT.-COL. H. M. SMAIL, T.D.
26th Field Company, Royal Engineers.
236th Field Company, Royal Engineers.
237th Field Company, Royal Engineers.
239th Field Park Company, Royal Engineers.

THE ROYAL CORPS OF SIGNALS: LT.-COL. T. P. E. MURRAY.
51st Divisional Signals Company.

THE ROYAL ARMY MEDICAL CORPS: A.D.M.S., LT.-COL. D. P. LEVACK.
152nd Field Ambulance.
153rd Field Ambulance.
154th Field Ambulance.

ORDER OF BATTLE

(*contd.*)

THE ROYAL ARMY SERVICE CORPS: LT.-COL. T. HARRIS-HUNTER, T.D.
Divisional Ammunition Company.
Divisional Petrol Company.
Divisional Supply Column.

ATTACHED TROOPS

51st Medium Regiment, Royal Artillery.
1st Royal Horse Artillery (less one Battery).
97th Field Regiment, Royal Artillery (one Battery).
213th Army Field Company, Royal Engineers.
1st Bn. Princess Louise's Kensington Regiment (Machine-Gunners).
7th Bn. The Royal Northumberland Fusiliers (Machine-Gunners).
6th Bn. The Royal Scots Fusiliers (Pioneers).
7th Bn. The Norfolk Regiment (Pioneers).
Sections of the Royal Army Ordnance Corps and the Royal Army Service Corps.

ARK FORCE

BRIGADIER A. C. L. STANLEY-CLARKE, D.S.O.

4th Bn. The Black Watch.
7th Bn. The Argyll & Sutherland Highlanders.
8th Bn. The Argyll & Sutherland Highlanders.
6th Bn. The Royal Scots Fusiliers (Pioneers).
4th Bn. The Border Regiment }
5th Bn. The Sherwood Foresters } "A" Brigade.
4th Bn. The Buffs }
1st Bn. Princess Louise's Kensington Regiment (less two Companies).
17th Field Regiment, Royal Artillery.
75th Field Regiment, Royal Artillery.
51st Anti-tank Regiment, Royal Artillery (one Battery).
236th Field Company, Royal Engineers.
237th Field Company, Royal Engineers.
239th Field Park Company, Royal Engineers.
154th Field Ambulance.

"I can tell you that the comradeship in arms experienced on the battlefield of Abbeville in May and June 1940 between the French Armoured Division, which I had the honour to command, and the valiant 51st Highland Division under General Fortune, played its part in the decision which I took to continue fighting on the side of the Allies unto the end no matter what may be the course of events."

GENERAL DE GAULLE at Edinburgh
20th June, 1942

ISSUED FOR THE WAR OFFICE
BY THE MINISTRY OF INFORMATION

THE

HIGHLAND

DIVISION

By ERIC LINKLATER

THE ARMY AT WAR

LONDON
HIS MAJESTY'S STATIONERY OFFICE
1942

MLRS
2004

CONTENTS

With four maps in line

THE HIGHLAND DIVISION

Author's Note

THE FRAMEWORK of this narrative was constructed of War Diaries of the Fifty-First Division and a table of movements compiled by Lt.-Colonel C. P. R. Johnston. For an obvious reason the War Diaries of most units were incomplete, but with the generous help of certain officers and men who were so fortunate and daring as to contrive their escape after being taken at St Valéry, I have been able to fill, in part at least, many gaps in the record. Other gaps remain, however, and I am conscious that to certain units justice has not been done. I know, for example, that somewhere between the Somme and the Bresle the 5th Gordons offered a most gallant and stubborn resistance to the enemy, but I could not describe the action because I know of only one surviving spectator, and he is now several thousand miles away.

But I am very grateful to the officers and men who have given me their help: in particular to Brigadier H. W. V. Stewart, who was tireless in assisting; to Lt.-Colonel A. Buchanan Smith, whose aid I first solicited; and to Brigadier A. C. L. Stanley-Clarke, who read and corrected the final draft. I have also to thank Lt.-Colonel Thomas Rennie, who endured cross-examination for eight consecutive hours, and Lt.-Colonel the Earl Cawdor, who suffered at least as long; Lt.-Colonel C. P. R. Johnston, whose table of movements was invaluable; Captain B. C. Bradford for a most vivid account of the last days, Major J. A. Hopwood, who showed me a long and admirable letter which his batman, Private McCready, had written to him, and Private McCready himself for permission to quote it; Lt.-Colonel R. W. Macintosh Walker, Captain C. W. Thomson, Captain Webb who shared the Argyll's escape from Ault, and Major Lorne Campbell for his excellent story of that escape; Major C. J. Y. Dallmeyer for two most useful reports, Second-Lieutenant Fullerton, Captain Sandford, and a number of N.C.O.'s and men of the Royal Corps of Signals who gave evidence with a clearness and detail that were a credit to their Corps; Mr. G. E. Ley Smith, of the Aberdeen *Press and Journal*, who had himself gathered much material and who lent me a very good narrative by an officer of the Royal Artillery; Mr. M. V. Hay of Seaton, Lt.-Colonel Scott-Elliot, and several others who contributed personal knowledge of various events.

The official opinion of the Division's performance during the battle of France can thus be judged by the fact that it has been reconstituted under its old name. The new 51st Division is in every way the equal of the old as the following tribute from the Secretary of State for War testifies.

"I should like you to know how much I enjoyed my day with the 51st Division. I was filled with comfort and admiration at all I saw and congratulate you and everybody else concerned at producing such a tiptop body. I wish you all the best of fortune and abundant opportunity for revenging your comrades and for adding new glories to an already glorious history."

1. The Fifty-First

TO THE Highland Territorials who composed the Fifty-First Division in the earlier German War, a strange thing happened: regimental loyalty—the normal sentiment of a soldier—was to a large extent replaced by their greater pride in the Division. Like other divisions with a consistently good record, it became corporate, and in a few years' time it acquired such a tradition as many a regiment has hardly won by a century of fortunate campaigning. Its quality was acknowledged, not only by English commanders and French allies, but by the enemy, while in Scotland its prowess became an accepted legend.

In the years of truce, when the Army was starved by Government and neglected by the people, many of the Highland battalions continued to recruit their full strength. The Fifty-First and its legend went on living, and when the Germans renewed their war against the civilised world, the Division mobilised, as well as men and officers, a fairly confident hope of winning new fame from its old enemy.

This hope was not realised. The Fifty-First, though separated from the British Expeditionary Force, shared its defeat. In May it was fighting near the Saar. It traversed France and came within sight of the sea. It fought before Abbeville and on the Bresle. Then, caught in the rout of the French, two of its brigades, or what remained of them, were trapped, on a morning of rain and the miscarriage of their plans, in the little town of St Valéry-en-Caux, and forced to surrender.

To Scotland the news came like another Flodden. Scotland is a small country, and in its northern half there was hardly a household that had not at least a cousin in one of the Highland regiments. The disaster, for a little while, seemed overwhelming, because, to begin with,

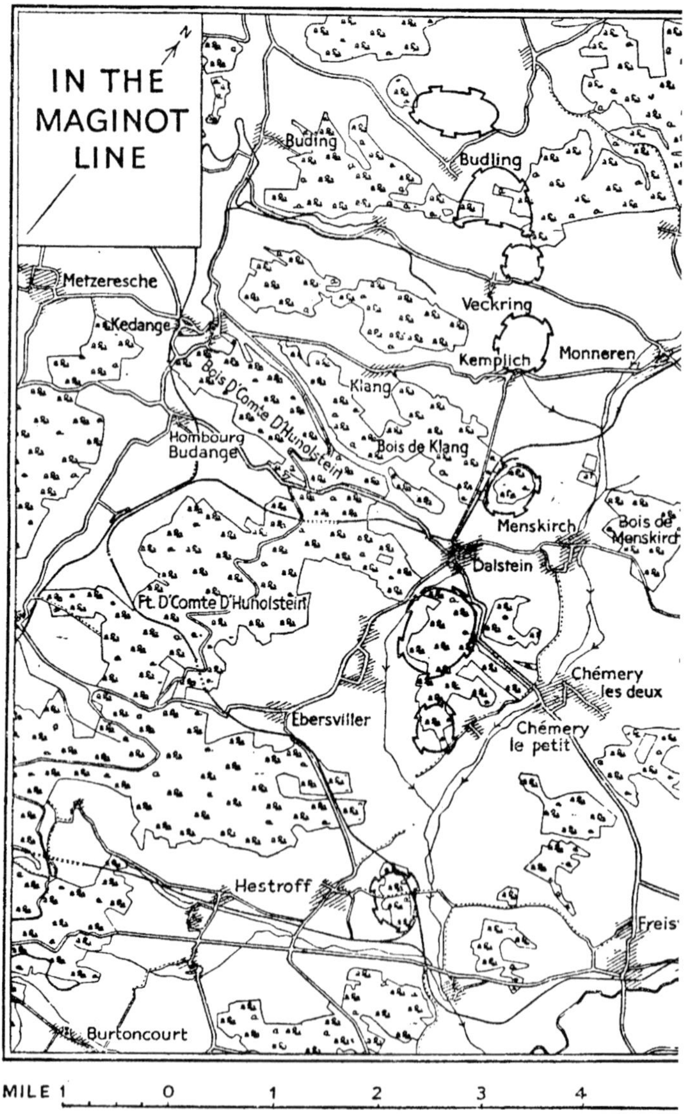
IN THE MAGINOT LINE
N
Buding
Budling
Metzeresche
Kedange
Veckring
Kemplich
Monneren
Bois D'Comte D'Hunolstein
Klang
Hombourg
Budange
Bois de Klang
Menskirch
Bois de Menskirch
Dalstein
Ft. D'Comte D'Hunolstein
Chémery les deux
Ebersviller
Chémery le petit
Hestroff
Burtoncourt
MILE 1 0 1 2 3 4

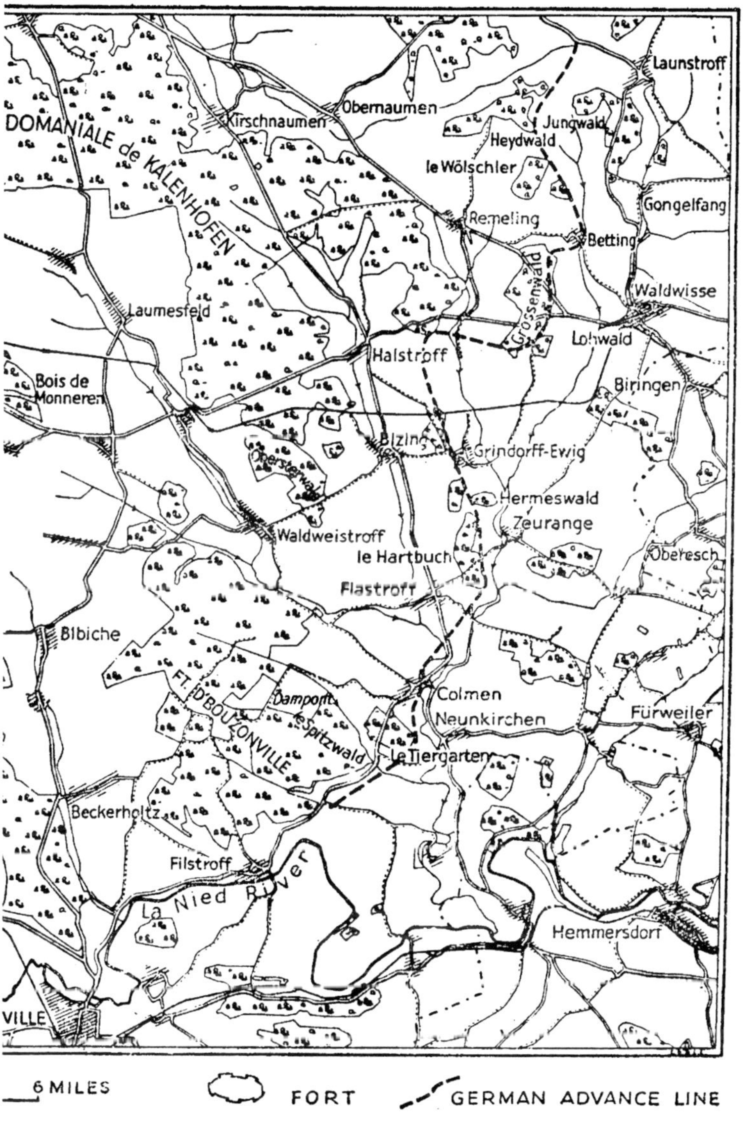

6 MILES   FORT   GERMAN ADVANCE LINE

nothing was known of the Division except the apparent shame of its surrender, and the undeniable capture of nearly six thousand men.

But the black morning at St Valéry does not tell the whole story. Before the Division walked into that disastrous trap it had fought well, endured with hardihood, and shown a youthful spirit that might have grown again to the victorious temper of Beaumont-Hamel. It failed indeed, but only in the grip of circumstances that made failure inevitable. Under the chalk-cliffs that overlook the Channel the legend of the Fifty-First went into eclipse, but not before it had gathered new substance on the river-banks of Normandy and Lorraine.

Normandy was frozen hard when, about the end of January 1940, the Fifty-First went ashore at Le Havre. Trees were sheathed in ice, the weight of it broke their branches, and the roads were armoured. A few days later came a thaw. Fog and rain obscured the country, while underfoot it melted deeply into mud. Then the frost returned.

The early weeks of foreign service were uncomfortable, and transport-drivers lived dangerously. The villainous weather prohibited most forms of training, but there was so much movement that everyone learnt by heart the tedious routine of military travel. Day after day they read in orders: "Breakfast will be consumed at 0700 hrs. and a haversack ration will be issued to all ranks. . . . Picks and shovels will be taken for digging latrines, scrubbing material for cleaning billets. O.C. 'A' Coy. will detail a fatigue party of 1 N.C.O. and 20 men to report to O. i/c loading at 0900 hrs. at Railway Station to distribute straw throughout the train."

The battalions moved towards the Belgian frontier, and were lodged in towns and villages with familiar names. Their French hosts were far more friendly than they had been a generation before, and the Highlanders did what they could to make a return of hospitality. Their Pipes and Drums played on occasion before the local Mairie; they collected money for the children of a kindly village; and now and then they gave a party. The Alliance had, so it seemed, more than political reason for its existence: there was mutual good feeling.

On March 28th the Division took over from the 21st French Division the line from Bailleul to Armentières, and set to work, with pick and shovel, with concrete-mixers and Dannert wire, on section-posts and platoon-positions. That was the day when the Supreme War Council of France and Britain made a solemn declaration of unity, and affirmed the intention of the two countries to fight as one, and live as one when fighting was finished.

2. Highlanders in the Maginot Line

IN THE early months of 1940, British formations, not larger than a brigade, were being attached for periods of fifteen days to the French Army in front of the Maginot Line. Service there offered useful experience. German patrols in the valley of the Saar were continually active, and men could be introduced to the sensation of being shot over. That was the purpose of attachment: not to relieve the French, but to acclimatise our new battalions to battle.

In April, however, it was decided that the British Army should take over a divisional sector on the Saar front, and the first and only division to be nominated for duty there was the Fifty-First. The Division had been reorganised, and now included three Regular battalions: the 1st Black Watch, the 1st Gordons, the 2nd Seaforths. These battalions had arrived in France within six weeks of our declaration of war, and the Black Watch had already done a tour in the forward defences of the Maginot system, spending Boxing Day, with frost and fog, in the *Ligne de Contact*.

The Maginot system included a lot more than its almost fabulous and quite futile concrete forts. In front of them lay what was known as *La Couverture*: the *Ligne de Contact*, which was roughly an outpost line; behind that, in many places, a *Ligne de Soutien*, or support line; and behind that the *Ligne de Recueil*. In the area of the Saar the *Ligne de Contact* was seven miles in front of the Maginot forts, and perhaps six miles from the forts of the Siegfried Line. The Maginot forts, or many of them, were also protected by what were known as *brisants*—strong infantry positions, projecting forward and designed to break and divert a frontal attack. And behind the forts there was an additional line of resistance—on paper, at least—the *Ligne d'Arrêt*.

The Fifty-First were allotted the sector about Hombourg-Budange, a cross-roads hamlet that lies between the Saar and the Moselle, some eighteen miles north-east of Metz. It is a rich green countryside of undulating hills, well watered by many streams, patched heavily with forest, sprinkled with orchards and numerous villages. The fields were wet, the ground soft, when the Highlanders arrived, but the weather was improving, and before long the midday sun was hot enough. After the bleak neighbourhood of Bailleul, bare and wintry, there was something like enchantment in the warmth and beauty of Lorraine. The woods were beech, and the huge pale trees were dressed in the brilliance of new leaves. The forest-floor was patched with lilies of the valley, and all the orchards were in bloom. Behind the forts there was still the foolish comfort of a land at peace. The people of Metz were dining well, dancing gaily, enjoying themselves. But the Fifty-First had work to do, for no army in the world can ever regard with full approval another's defensive system, but must always deepen what has been dug, site guns anew, and re-wire perimeters.

Outposts in the Saar Valley

It was in the third week of April that the Fifty-First took train for the Saar front, and by May 1st, with their attached troops, they had relieved the French at Hombourg-Budange; the 154th Brigade, first on the field, had already had their turn in the front line, and the 1st Black Watch had been in action. They had beaten off a small but fierce attack on some posts in the *Ligne de Contact*, about the fringes of Hartbuch Wood. Our outpost line consisted of platoon-posts among the woods from Heydwald to the Grossenwald, from the village of Remeling to Grindorff-Ewig, to the Hartbuch and through Flastroff towards Neunkirchen, which the Germans held.

The typical platoon-post comprised a group of what appeared to be log-cabins within a dense perimeter of barbed-wire. About the fringes of the woods the ground was so wet that it had been scarcely possible to dig positions into it: they had had to be built on top of it. The log-cabins had been constructed by the French, and unfortunately they were not bullet-proof. In open ground there were field trenches, sand-bagged and revetted, but the French had created many more positions than the Fifty-First could hold, or thought desirable; and the surplus ones had to be flattened, or the Germans might occupy them. The two Pioneer battalions, the Royal Scots Fusiliers and the Norfolks, were kept busy and did some strenuous work. Forward of the Maginot forts they used mules to carry their building material. This was the only form of transport that could be taken right into the outpost line, and though the mules were sometimes temperamental, they served their purpose well. With remarkable speed the log-cabins were replaced by dug-in positions of a more serviceable sort.

The forward view from the *Ligne de Contact* was stopped by a wooded ridge about a mile away. The countryside, beneath its greenery, wore a strange look of suspended animation, for the many villages in front of the Maginot Line, though they stood unharmed, had all been evacuated. Empty houses stood on vacant streets, and all the windows were shuttered.

But though the villages were deserted, the woods, in a furtive way, were still populous. Some of them were virgin forest, unthinned, almost impassable. The 4th Seaforths, beating Bouzonville Wood in mid-May, were amazed by the wild and curious noises that came from its depths. A soldier, leaping into the undergrowth, caught a wildly squealing pig. Another came out hugging a young barking-deer. The wild animals in the wood were very noisy indeed, but the German soldiers who lay hidden there were silent fellows. There were always some Germans in Bouzonville Wood.

The battalions took their turn in the *Ligne de Contact*, and the skirmishing there grew fiercer. A typical encounter would start with a few shots fired from the darkness into a platoon-post, or the throwing of a grenade at a figure seen dimly in a forest ride, and from its explosion might flare a miniature battle. Very lights, splitting the darkness, would reveal the enemy beyond the coiling wire. If the attack were pushed, and reinforced, the green-and-white lights of an S O S would bring a defensive curtain of artillery-fire, or might summon the comforting noise of Bren-carriers. Our dawn patrols, searching the woods, would see where some German had lain wounded, or fallen dead.

By day and night there was unremitting attention to the enemy's movement, and everything was reported that might be a clue to his purpose or dispositions. A working-party of five men come over such-and-such a ridge, carrying corrugated iron-sheets. . . . At 1800 hrs.

enemy working-parties finish for the day. . . . Heavy transport is heard by a patrol from the direction of Waldwisse. . . . There are bird-calls, quickly answered, very frequent, moving to the rear. . . . Four shells come over: time of flight 10 secs. . . . There is movement in the wire of 3 men and a dog near No. 4 post. . . . Noises like an owl, in an orchard. . . . Two upstairs windows of white house, extreme left of Biringen, open to-day for the first time. . . . There was a pole and stick, carrying barbed-wire head-high, across the stream. . . . Flastroff church-tower —but this comes later—is said to be occupied by the enemy: the clock hands are revolving.

Routine Patrol

The German troops who held the advanced positions of the Siegfried Line had the great advantage of knowing the country. Many were local men who had poached the woods they now patrolled, and were familiar with every yard of the ground. Their patrols were aggressive, and dominated the area. On a front so thinly held it was impossible to keep them out, and sometimes they penetrated as far as Waldweistroff. They made much use of trained dogs, and of tricks to unnerve the defence: such as removing from the wire of a platoon-perimeter the empty tins strung upon it to give warning of trespassers.

The French had inclined to an attitude of live and let live, but the Fifty-First was more active. Patrols went out to hamper and observe the enemy, to provoke him to fight. It was the Divisional policy that the routine patrol should be carried out in so enterprising a fashion as to make deliberate raiding unnecessary, and the nightly stalking of the enemy—with grenade and tommy-gun, the patrol with their faces blackened—was done with persistent energy and a high spirit. Here, for example, is an illuminating report by Second-Lieutenant A. L. Orr

Ewing of the 7th Argyll and Sutherlands, who led a fighting patrol:

"I left our own wire near F 9 in the Grossenwald at 2300 hrs., and made my way to the S.E. corner of the Lohwald. I lay-up in the trees on the rt. hand side. About 0130 hrs. I heard someone moving in the wood, and 10 minutes later more movement. I lay quiet for 5 minutes and then decided to investigate. I left 4 men with 2 automatic guns in the trees to cover me, and also to shoot anyone trying to leave the corner of the wood. With the remaining men I moved forward between the stream and the wood. About 40 yds. away from me I saw 3 men running from the wood towards the stream. I opened fire with my sub-machine gun, and two men dropped. Heavy firing from at least 4 tommy-guns immediately opened on my flash. My patrol and I all dropped flat, and continued to fire and throw grenades. About 8 or 10 men then left the wood and opened fire. More men in the wood also fired on us. One man advanced towards us, but was severely hit in the stomach. At least two more were hit by grenades, as we heard them screaming. The enemy threw stick-grenades, one landing near my batman and me, cutting us both, and temporarily blinding me with blood. Owing to the superior numbers of the enemy, and the fact that our ammunition was running low, we withdrew about 60 yds. under covering fire from the 4 men we had left in our rear. The enemy then also withdrew, and we heard them talking on the other side of the stream. As it was then our time to return, we made our way back to our own wire."

3. The Affair of Grossenwald

ON MAY 7TH the 4th Black Watch took over the *Ligne de Contact* in the neighbourhood of Remeling from the 1st Gordons. There were French troops on their left and the

154th Brigade on their right. Their Battalion Headquarters were in Remeling, their companies along the forward edges of the woods of Heydwald, the Wölschler, and the Grossenwald. There was, to begin with, no more than normal activity, but on May 10th came the *mise en garde*: the Germans had begun their attack on the Low Countries, and along the whole front the war quickened.

Two days later, in the early afternoon, a Company Commander of the 4th Black Watch set out for the village of Betting. His battalion was due to be relieved by the 5th Gordons, and a Gordon officer went with him. They did not anticipate trouble, and were surprised when, from the wood, a German machine-gun opened fire on them. Betting, it appeared, was out of bounds, and a few hours later came the news that the village was surrounded, and the Black Watch platoon that held it was being heavily attacked. Some carriers were sent up to help, and the Germans withdrew. On the following morning, at five minutes past four, the enemy began to fire a heavy barrage along the whole battalion front, and the 154th Brigade's front to the right. To the right of the Divisional front, the Germans attacked and took some French positions. The Allied artillery replied. Behind the enemy's barrage came infantry armed with grenades, automatic guns, and flame-throwers. They made some progress round the right of the Grossenwald, but Heydwald and the Wölschler were held, and the lonely section that remained in Betting—surrounded and shelled again—was still lively. About nine o'clock at night, when the village was in flames, this section was rescued by Second-Lieutenant Rhodes leading a fighting patrol of the 1st Gordons.

A company of the Black Watch, its communications cut, put up an S O S about half-past five the next morning: it had held off for more than an hour a determined infantry attack, but now it was hard pressed. A troop of the Lothians and Border Horse (Yeomanry) was sent to investigate, but one of its tanks was bogged in the soft ground about the fringes of the Grossenwald, and the other two were hit by anti-tank fire and high explosive. Enemy machine-guns and mortars were in action in the Hermeswald, their artillery was still lively, and some of our posts had been badly knocked about by eight-inch shells. A report came through that the Germans were concentrating about Zeurange, another that they had broken through the 4th Black Watch. A company of Argyll and Sutherlands was sent to cover the gap, but found it was not needed: the 4th were holding on. Young soldiers in their first engagement, they held their positions with commendable endurance.

Before midnight the 4th Black Watch had been relieved—all but one company, which was still in difficulties—and the 5th Gordons were in the line. Watching them go forward, their Colonel, Buchanan Smith, was "very much struck by the seriousness in their faces, and how they put their confidence in the officers. I wondered how many would ever again possess those boyish faces." To their right were the 1st Black Watch, and according to a letter written by Private J. McCready, of that regiment, they had a profitable tour. They suffered perhaps a dozen casualties, but inflicted more. McCready, talking of his friends, says that "Price and Fisher had an excellent time with a Bren gun and a rifle, their bag of the enemy was put down as 44 in an afternoon. It was all storm-troopers in that action, but the Black Watch was more than a match for them, they proved nothing better than good target practice as some of the boys said."

The Germans had no Gaelic

To the right of the Black Watch, from the east corner of Hartbuch to the north edge of Spitzwald were the 4th Seaforths, who had newly relieved the 4th Camerons.

The Camerons had had a roughish time, losing a couple of section-posts in the Tiergarten, and the Brigade battle-patrol had been isolated by fire in Spitzwald. The Germans, who made a practice of tapping our forward telephone cables, were sadly disappointed by the Camerons, who countered this form of espionage by talking with their platoon-posts in Gaelic. And before being relieved, the Camerons had retaken some of their lost positions.

During the early morning of the 14th, in the Gordons sector, the Germans fired 3,600 shells into a company front within an hour and a half: forty shells a minute, or thereabout. Telephone cables and defensive wire were cut, and German infantry followed the barrage. But the Gordons fought them off, and the Black Watch, on their right, noted the large number of dead in front of one of their posts. The 1st Black Watch were now being relieved by the 7th Argyll and Sutherlands. They had lost six killed and seventeen wounded, but on the wire about one of their platoon positions they counted thirteen German bodies, and the night before, when quietness came with dusk, they had watched the enemy carrying his dead from the Grossenwald. The guns of the 17th Field Regiment, Royal Artillery, had done good work in the sector.

This was the day on which Holland surrendered.

"D" company of the 5th Gordons, on the extreme left of the front at Heydwald, had lost touch with two of its forward posts, and patrols sent over to re-establish contact were driven back by heavy machine-gun fire. At five o'clock on the morning of the 15th, the Germans enclosed three posts of "D" company, as if in a box, by concentrated artillery fire. At six o'clock their infantry attacked, and was driven off. Then the barrage came down again, and for another three hours the shelling lasted. No news came from the forward posts, and every attempt to reconnoitre was driven back by machine-gun fire. Later in the day "D" company reported it was holding its last position with twenty-eight men, and the wire was down. But the Company Commander was still thinking of his lost platoons, and how to get to them. He was imprisoned by the fire of automatic weapons, and sent a request for tommy-guns to deal with them. He wanted tommy-guns to fight forward, with his twenty-eight survivors, and look for his lost men.

But the forward posts had been captured, and "D" company, with nearly seventy casualties, had to withdraw under the covering fire of a fighting patrol. Its withdrawal preceded by only a few hours the withdrawal of the whole Division.

It had become evident that our advanced positions were untenable against the superior forces which the Germans were using. According to a French statement, based on the identification of casualties, they had employed more than a dozen units in the recent attack, and both troops and weapons had been selected for the purpose from the garrison of the Siegfried Line. The estimate of numbers, however, was probably inaccurate: many of the German troops belonged to the Schutzstaffel, who carry, in addition to their S.S. papers, a record of their previous regiments, and this double identification may have misled the French intelligence officers. But the attack was undoubtedly a serious offensive movement, and after consultation with General Condé, General Fortune had decided to abandon Heydwald, the Grossenwald, the Wölschler and Betting village, and form a new line along the ridge of Kalenhofen. But before this movement had begun, withdrawal was ordered to the *Ligne de Recueil.* It was necessary to make this deep retirement to conform with the movements of the French on either flank, where the Germans were pushing hard.

Elan and Staunchness

To evacuate positions so near to the enemy's fluid line was by no means easy—a company of the 7th Argylls lost two sergeants and seven men, killed by shell-fire; a company of the 5th Gordons slipped out of the Wölschler, covered by a sergeant of the Kensingtons and his two machine-guns—and the defences of the *Ligne de Recueil* were by no means complete. It lay about three miles in front of the Maginot Line, on a forward slope. The field of fire was good, but the wire was thin, communication trenches were poor, and an anti-tank ditch had been only half-dug. The Germans, however, did not press their advance. Extensive demolitions had been prepared along the Divisional front, and beside every charge two Sappers had waited patiently for the blessed order to blow. It came—and roads went skyward, bridges collapsed, trees tumbled. The German advance was usefully impeded: they came no farther than the Obsterwald.

For a few more days the battalions were shuffled and dealt among the rearward lines, the woods and villages of the Saar front. They lay in a forest, or dug slit-trenches. The Sappers filled minefields for tanks, and improved the *brisants* at Chémery le Petit, and in the Kalenhofen Forest. A fighting patrol of the 7th Argylls went out and found a German officer in the attic of a house, bombed another out of its cellar. The Lothians became infantry and held a sector of the front till the French relieved them on May 22nd.

But all this was mere temporising. The Division had come to the end of its short term of service in Lorraine, and was waiting its order for some other front. It had no reason to be disappointed with itself. In action for the first time, it had behaved well, and the French General Condé, commanding the Third Army, had spoken of its high fighting qualities and high morale. "The Highlanders of 1940," he said, "have renewed the tradition of Beaumont-Hamel."

This was courtesy indeed, but the courtesy had been earned. The Division had already shown something of its traditional *élan*, and, for troops at their baptism of fire, their defence of the outpost line had been most staunch and resolute. To savour the individual quality of the men, consider these reports of action in the Grossenwald. Here is Platoon Sergeant-Major Fullerton of the 5th Gordons: "On 14th May, Stand To and Stand Down normal. After Stand Down Boche started shelling. After 2 hours it died down. I took a patrol back to Coy. H.Q. and chased a couple of skulking Germans. The distance to Coy. H.Q. was about 400 yards. Then on Capt. Lawrie's orders I took a patrol to 16 Pl. on the left to 2/Lt. Langham who reported everything O.K. but bothered with snipers from Bois Carré. On getting back to 17 Pl. extreme left section commander just in front of Bois Carré had a man wounded by snipers in tree. I got both snipers fixed with Bren gun. Breakfasts in containers from Coy. H.Q. Bn. Intelligence Officer, 2/Lt. Morrison, arrived up and I helped him establish a post in Bois Carré. We found about 25 Germans there and killed them all. They were behind a hedge. We patrolled right through and took identity papers, etc., from the corpses and took back 2 German L.M.G.'s."

And here is a Company Commander in the 1st Black Watch: "There was a heavy barrage on the three section posts. S O S from left, and then from Command Post. I crawled with my runner to the right post, where the men stated they had shot a number of Boches. The attitude of this section was most aggressive. They had put three Boche machine-guns out of action. While I was there a German, presumably the commander of the attacking party, was shouting a great deal. The platoon commander distributed ammunition which I had brought up. At the left-hand post I found the enemy on three sides, but they had not penetrated the wire. At 1500 hrs. the 7th A. & S.H. fighting patrol arrived: Orr Ewing and three men went out and brought in a German machine-gun, 500 rounds, a sniper's rifle and three bodies. German casualties here were estimated at forty."

Both on the Saar front and later in Normandy, the two machine-gun battalions—Northumberland Fusiliers and Kensingtons—were for tactical purposes divided among the Brigades, and because they did not fight as a whole it is difficult to assess or describe their work. But wherever the infantry were in action there were machine-gunners to support them, and perhaps it is sufficient to say that the battalions which had Kensingtons attached to them speak well of the Kensingtons, while those which were assisted by the Northumberland Fusiliers were convinced that they had the better support. The conclusion is that both were good.

4. The Division Moves Westward

ON MAY 20TH the Fifty-First went into reserve to a French army-group, and was ordered to the neighbourhood of Etain, some twenty miles north-west of Metz. The movement, from Hombourg-Budange to Etain, was completed on May 22nd, and before dawn broke on the 23rd, the 154th Brigade was on its way to Varennes, north-west of Verdun, followed a few hours later by the Lothians. There was news that the Germans had broken through west of Montmédy, and the Fifty-First was being sent to meet them. By daylight on May 25th, all who could be moved by motor-transport were concentrated in the Grandpré–Varennes area, and the remainder had entrained and were on their way.

By this time the battle of France had been split in two,

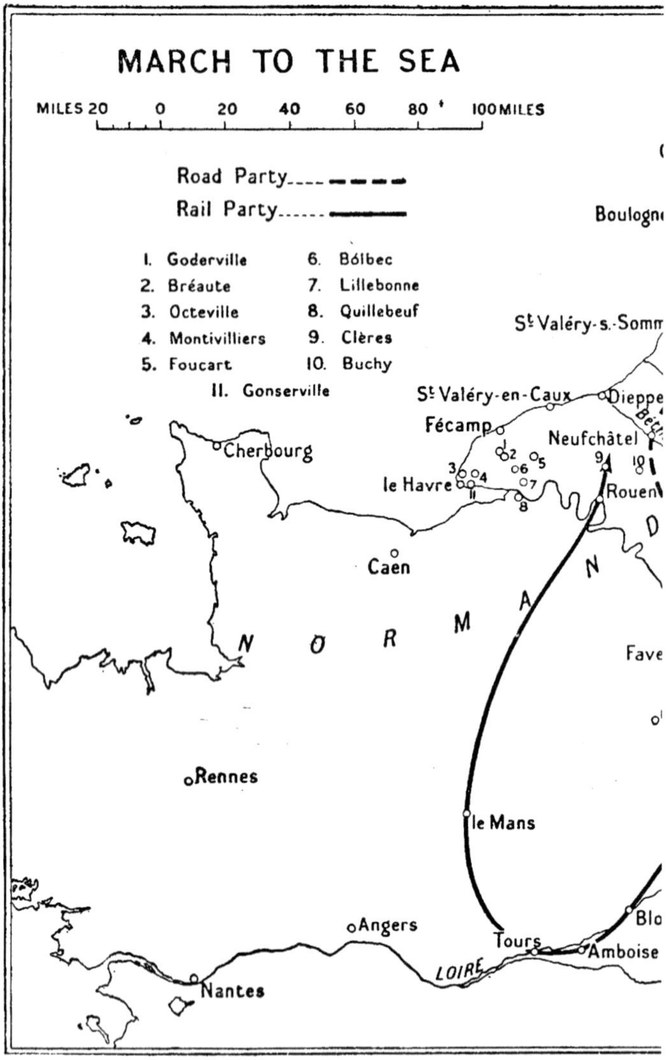
MARCH TO THE SEA
MILES 20 0 20 40 60 80 100 MILES
Road Party
Rail Party
1. Goderville
2. Bréaute
3. Octeville
4. Montivilliers
5. Foucart
6. Bólbec
7. Lillebonne
8. Quillebeuf
9. Clères
10. Buchy
11. Gonserville
St Valéry-en-Caux
Fécamp
Neufchâtel
Cherbourg
le Havre
Rouen
Caen
N O R M A N D
Rennes
le Mans
Angers
Tours
Amboise
LOIRE
Nantes

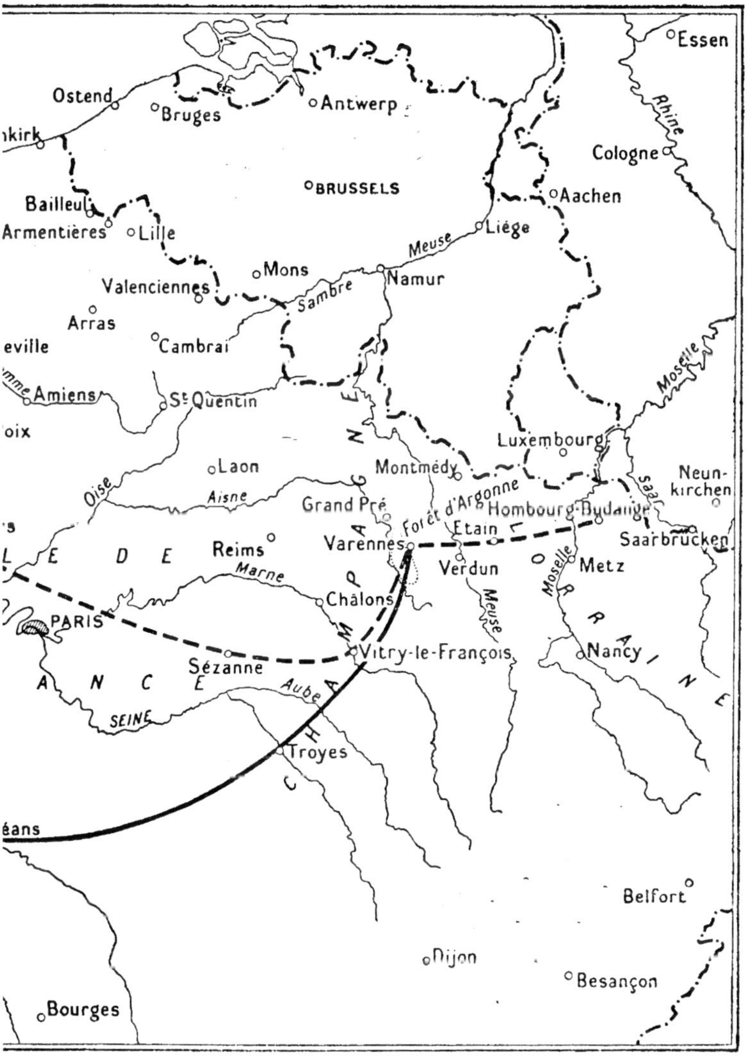

Essen
Rhine
Cologne
Ostend
Bruges
Antwerp
BRUSSELS
Aachen
Bailleul
Armentières
Lille
Liége
Meuse
Mons
Namur
Valenciennes
Sambre
Arras
Cambrai
Amiens
St Quentin
Moselle
Luxembourg
Montmédy
Laon
Oise
Aisne
Grand Pré
Forêt d'Argonne
Hombourg-Budange
Neun-kirchen
Saar
Etain
Reims
Varennes
Saarbrücken
Metz
Verdun
Marne
Châlons
Moselle
Meuse
PARIS
Vitry-le-François
Nancy
Sézanne
Aube
SEINE
Troyes
CHAMPAGNE
LORRAINE
Belfort
Dijon
Besançon
Bourges

and the Germans were pouring their motorised divisions through the widening gap between Arras and the Somme to spill them against the Channel ports. The Guards had been driven out of Boulogne, and the Riflemen of Calais were fighting their desperate battle against time and two Panzer divisions. In the north the British Expeditionary Force and the Belgian Army were steadily withdrawing: the area of battle was shrinking westward to the coast. There was confused and furious fighting between Valenciennes and Cambrai and Arras.

The first intention of the Grand Quartier-Général had been to use the Fifty-First in the defence of Paris. Then, more urgently, the danger seemed to come from Montmédy, and the Division was ordered to Varennes. But it did not stay. There was a day when plans were changeable as April weather, and every command was hotly pursued by countermand. Even before leaving the Saar, the Officer Commanding the 6th Royal Scots Fusiliers had discovered a certain indecision in higher ranks. In search of information, he had asked the Colonel of the 7th Argyll and Sutherlands what news he had of intended movement; the latter gravely answered that the Corporal in charge of the Divisional Concert Party had just assured him they would remain where they were. A few days later the Fusiliers' Colonel records in his diary: "We reached Verdun in order to be told we were going to Le Mans."

Then the Division went to Normandy, and the rail-parties that were slowly moving towards Varennes were diverted to Rouen; the road-parties turned their transport westward to the sea. Their route was by Vitry le François, Sézanne and Gisors—from Lorraine through Champagne and the Ile de France—then north-westward to Neufchâtel, where they make cream-cheese in the shape of a bung, and so to the battlefield of the three rivers—the Somme and the Bresle and the Béthune. On May 30th the

Colonel of the Royal Scots Fusiliers records with a brief satisfaction: "'C' Company had trout for dinner, caught in a dry-fly stream passing the door of their billet."

Mechanised Migration

The Divisional transport and the lorry-borne troops travelled about three hundred miles of French roads. In peace time, in a civilian car whose driver has only his private responsibility, such a journey would be neither remarkable nor difficult. But the movement of soldiers is never a simple operation, and the Fifty-First's march to the sea was made against time, in a country stupefied by sudden invasion, over roads that were roughly parallel to the German corridor and no more than thirty-odd miles away from it. From the Forest of Argonne, where men, wagons and guns had lain hidden among the trees, to the Haute Forêt d'Eu, where they assembled for battle, was a three-days' journey in drill-order: over an indicated route, at an ordered speed, in a fixed density of so many vehicles to the mile. Supply points and staging areas had to be arranged. Advanced-parties must be told off, road-pickets detailed, motor-cyclists sent forward at such-and-such a time. The huge assortment of vehicles—there were about three thousand of one sort or another—had to be marshalled according to their purpose and their kind: troop-carriers and Bren-carriers, company vehicles and cooking trucks, blanket lorries in the transport echelon, water-trucks, utility-trucks, and trucks mounting light machine-guns for anti-aircraft defence. The migration of an Asiatic tribe, with all its flocks and herds in search of summer pasture, is a simple matter when compared with the time-tabled movement of Divisional transport through an invaded country; but the movement was completed speedily and without appreciable loss. As far as Paris the roads were almost empty, but throughout the journey drivers were troubled by great clouds of dust, and despatch-riders with inflamed eyes were temporarily blinded by it. Yet barely half a dozen vehicles were lost. Some idea of the problem of fuel supply may appear in the fact that during the final month of its existence the Division's *average* petrol-consumption was sixteen thousand gallons a day.

The train parties took a long route south of Paris. They too went to Vitry le François, where, according to an officer of the 8th Argylls, "the train stopped, as a French ammunition-train in the station had been hit by a German bomb about ten minutes before our arrival, and was still in the process of exploding." When the ammunition-wagons had finished their *feu de joie*, the troop-trains went on and fetched a great circle by the Loire; and through open doors in summer weather the men could see among the trees the walls and turrets of the châteaux of Orléans and Blois, Amboise and Tours. Then they turned north to Le Mans and Rouen, left the railway and took to the roads and the Norman woods. French buses bore them forward, buses that were battered and bruised, fore and aft, by frequent collision, and pitted with numerous bullet-holes. The drivers, French civilians, drove at a furious pace, and the column was directed by a French subaltern—with a megaphone—in a small Citroën that travelled more furiously still. This, providentially, was a day of heavy mist and pouring rain, the only bad weather the Division had till its last day came with a more wretched dawning. The long column, grouped far too closely on the open road, was protected from German bombers by cloud-cover and the low sky: sixty miles were covered without mishap.

By cornfield and soaking pasture, by dripping orchard and dales that were full of mist, the Division advanced. Over the hedgerows loomed the spire of a village church, or the shadowy chancel of a ruined abbey. Above a river, pocked with the rain, stood the square keep of a fallen castle, and heavy trees disappeared in cloud over the low hills. Down the weeping roads, drenched and miserable, came refugees fleeing from the north.

Basques and de Gaulle

First flight of the Division—152nd Brigade—arrived in the Haute Forêt d'Eu, overlooking the river Bresle, on May 28th. There the Camerons found the very gallant fragment of a Basque regiment. The Basques had come back from Breda in Holland. They numbered a Captain, four subalterns, and a hundred and fifty other ranks. Addressing them in Blangy, their Captain told them that he proposed to hold the line of the Bresle from Blangy to Gamaches. Because of their heavy casualties in Holland, he said, they were in the happy position of having a very high proportion of *mitrailleuses* and *fusils mitrailleurs*, with plenty of ammunition and abundance of wine. They would hold the shallow Bresle for ever, he declared.

The Highlanders and the men from the Pyrenees got on very well together, and the Camerons gave their Allies some anti-tank weapons to stiffen their resistance. That night, after a day of rain, of conference in the forest, and the news that Belgium had surrendered, the 4th Seaforths went forward to Le Transloy, three miles beyond the river, their Commanding Officer, Lieut.-Colonel Houldsworth, having assembled his battalion and completed his reconnaissance between mid-afternoon and late evening. By the following day the whole Division had assembled on a front extending from Senarpont to Eu. On its right, at Senarpont, was the French IX Corps; on its left, at Eu, it was supposed to be in contact with French marines. The Division was to hold approximately twenty miles.

The Germans had by this time crossed the Somme in the vicinity of Abbeville, and established bridgeheads—a smallish one at St Valéry-sur-Somme, a large one opposite Abbeville, where they held a triangular territory of which the apex was Huppy, and the river from Petit Port to Pont Rémy the base. In the early morning of May 29th a joint attack was made on the Abbeville bridgehead by our 1st Armoured Division and the French, under French command. The attack was not synchronised, and the Armoured Division suffered heavily and achieved none of its purpose; but the French won a partial success, and pushed back the apex of the German triangle to a point between Miannay and Moyenneville. The French tank-commander was General de Gaulle.

Brigadier Stewart, commanding the 152nd Brigade, who was reconnoitring an area east of the battle, found himself without intention an intimate spectator of it. He was surrounded by its overflow. The tanks moving hither and thither, jerkily, with sudden rushes, were strangely reminiscent of insects darting across the surface of a pond. In spite of gun-fire, the éclat of bursting shells, the spectacle appeared curiously unreal. War, which had once been a solid thing, had become almost entirely fluid.

On the following day the French again attacked, with infantry, tanks and bombers. Three squadrons made a determined assault on Abbeville, but met a dense barrage of light anti-aircraft fire, while the infantry and tanks failed to make any deeper impression on the bridgehead. "B" company of the 1st Black Watch—on loan from the 153rd Brigade—took part in this attack, and the men were exasperated by its failure. The battalion had spent the previous day moving forward, under orders repeatedly altered, to destinations which varied accordingly. Finally, in the early hours of the 30th, they relieved French cavalry at Miannay, Bouillancourt and Toeuffles; and at two o'clock in the afternoon "B" company was ordered to take the Grand Bois of Cambron at a quarter-past four. It went out and met machine-gun fire from the right; it destroyed this opposition. In the wood it met with no resistance and arrived at its objective on the north-eastern outskirts. But because the French attack on the village of Cambron was unsuccessful, the Black Watch was left with a flank in the air and had to retire to come into line with its neighbours.

Shortly before midnight de Gaulle informed Brigadier Stewart that he was doubtful if he could hold the villages of Moyenneville and Bienfay, that he had won the day before. For some time, indeed, Moyenneville was very scantily occupied, though the French colonel who commanded the area walked up and down the streets, magnificently unperturbed by the near neighbourhood of the enemy and the poverty of his garrison. Stewart agreed to reinforce this pair of villages immediately, and sent up the 2nd Seaforths, who moved with so little delay that by six o'clock in the morning two companies were in Bienfay, two in Moyenneville; the remainder of the Brigade 4th Camerons and 4th Seaforths—being at Limeux and Béhen.

The Line of the Somme

On May 31st General Altmayer, commanding the French IX Corps, ordered the Fifty-First to hold the line of the Somme from Erondelle to the sea. The French had originally undertaken to eliminate the Abbeville bridgehead before handing over the sector to us. They had failed to do this, and General Fortune's position was more difficult than he had anticipated. But the 152nd Brigade immediately relieved the French in the villages it had already reinforced; and on June 1st brigade frontages were allotted among the woods and hamlets on the south bank of the Somme, with the 152nd Brigade on the right, the 153rd in the centre, and the 154th on the left.

Many of the French troops had already been in battle, and were short of equipment. The 5th Light Cavalry, for instance, whose sector was taken over by the 154th Brigade, had fought through the campaign in Belgium, where they had lost all but two of their armoured cars. But they had saved their guns, and with these salvaged weapons, after a hurried move, they had held their position on the Somme.

The Armoured Division had withdrawn to the neighbourhood of Rouen to refit, leaving a support-group of one brigade which, with the Lothians and Border Horse, was placed in Divisional reserve. But within a few hours the Lothians had to take over a position from the French, and were in the front line, on the extreme right of it, from Erondelle to Tourbières. If it was to hold a front of twenty miles or more, the Fifty-First could scarcely afford the luxury of an adequate Divisional reserve.

Preparation was made for a new attack on the Abbeville bridgehead. There was no certain knowledge of the strength of the German position, and though the enemy had been able to deal heavy damage to our Armoured Division, and wholly to repulse the second French attack, a report was current that so far the bridgehead was only lightly held. But the Germans were bringing up reinforcements, and their obvious intention was to continue their offensive from the salient they had created; if they were to be attacked, then the sooner the better.

General de Gaulle's command had now left the lower Somme for service elsewhere, but the infantry, tanks and guns of the French 31st Division had arrived on the Bresle. A considerable strength of artillery, French and British, was brought into position, and ammunition dumped on the battery sites. The attack would be supported by about two hundred and fifty guns of all calibres, and the conference to elaborate a fire-plan lasted for more than three hours. It was complicated by the fact that none of the French officers spoke much English, and few of the British officers had more than twenty words of French. Finally it was decided that the French attack would be supported by French artillery, the British by their own guns.

Seventy miles away, while this battle of the rivers was being mounted, the last remaining fragments of the British Expeditionary Force were ferried home from the nightmare beaches of Dunkirk. . . .

5. The Battle of Abbeville

AT FIVE O'CLOCK on the afternoon of June 3rd the road from Blangy to St Maxent was closed to the Fifty-First to allow the French to bring forward their troops, tanks and guns from the Bresle. The battle would begin at dawn; or so it was hoped. But ammunition for the French 75's was late in arriving, and the attack, it seemed, would have to be postponed. All through the short night the road from Blangy was fearfully congested, but before daylight came it was clear again, and the 75's had their complement of shells. At three o'clock on June 4th the Allied artillery opened intensive fire on the German positions, and half an hour later tanks and infantry, French and Scots, advanced towards their first objective.

Their goal was about six miles of ground overlooking the water-meadows from Caubert on the right to the Cambron woods on their left. The 4th Camerons, on the right, would attack Caubert and the wooded ridge called the Hedgehog. In the centre the French with their tanks, and the 4th Seaforths under French command, would make for the Roman fort on the north end of the Mont de Caubert, and try to clear all the country between the two main roads that lead to Abbeville. And the 1st Gordons, on the left, would from Cahon attack the Cambron woods and the spur overlooking Cambron. The task of the 154th Brigade, on the extreme left, was to prevent the enemy from reinforcing his bridgehead. The Brigade was given no objective to capture.

The Germans, by unlucky coincidence, had also mounted an attack for the morning of the 4th, and on their left—our right—their infantry moved out a few minutes before our barrage opened. When "B" company of the 4th Camerons advanced towards the Hedgehog, they encountered, in a field of rye well in front of the hill, a German battalion quite unscathed by gun-fire. There was stern fighting there. The Germans had sited numerous machine-guns in the corn, and "B" company had many casualties. One officer survived, Second-Lieutenant Robertson, who led the remaining forty of the company into a wood north-west of Mareuil–Caubert, where "A" company was waiting. There he reorganised his command, and returning to Battalion Headquarters at Huchenneville asked for more ammunition that he might resume his attack on the Hedgehog. But when he revealed his strength, he was dissuaded of his ambition.

"D" company, on the left, went forward against Caubert, and also met German infantry. The two right-hand platoons fought their way through and the fifty men who survived, under Second-Lieutenant David Ross, made good their objective. The other platoons, advancing along the Route Nationale, met intense machine-gun fire from the road ahead of them, and from the dominating ridge of the Mont de Caubert, where the French had failed to capture Cæsar's Camp.

In the centre the attack was led by a battalion of French heavy tanks and a battalion of Chasseurs portés. Most of the tanks were wrecked, either by mines in a previously undetected minefield, or by anti-tank guns which had not been observed until they opened fire. A few tanks reached their objective, but had to retire to refuel, or were driven off again: the Germans had dug their guns deep into the chalky vallum of the Roman camp, and only a long-continued, densely-concentrated bombardment could have silenced them. Some of the French motorised infantry got as far as Yonval, in the valley west of the Caubert ridge, but were unable to go farther or to hold their ground.

The Seaforths Went On

The second wave of the attack consisted of a battalion of French light tanks and the leading companies of the 4th Seaforths. Advancing from the wooded slopes east of Bienfay, they approached the naked rise of the Mont de Caubert. But the tanks endured no more than two or three hundred yards of open country. Mines blew them up, or gun-fire hit and disabled them. The French officers and tank-crews were cheerful, confident, and superbly brave. They saw their leaders hit and disabled, but without doubt or hesitation followed, steering their vehicles into the deadly fire of the German anti-tank guns, till they too were killed. Their tanks lay inert and useless, or burst into flame. They were all put out of action.

The Seaforths went on without them. They ran into withering machine-gun fire, and were mown like grass. But those who lived went on, and the attack was carried a little farther. Some survivors reached their first objective, about six hundred yards up the slope. They were few in number. Sergeant Donald MacLeod was the only man left of his platoon. When his officer was killed, MacLeod led the platoon. Man after man fell to the clattering machine-guns that cut them down like a reaper. MacLeod himself, badly wounded, went on alone.

When Major Simon Fraser, commanding "B" company, was last seen, he was making a forward reconnaissance. Though his company was almost annihilated, he was still intent on reaching his objective. He refused to admit the evidence of defeat that lay so abundantly on the ridge, and went on. But there was only a handful of men to follow, and on his left and below him were the French infantry at Yonval, incapable of advancing till the Mont de Caubert had been won. And of the tanks that should have led the way to Cæsar's Camp, not one remained.

The 2nd Seaforths were successful, taking one of the Bienfay woods, and on the left "C" company of the 1st Gordons advanced from Cahon in face of stiff opposition from enemy machine-gun posts, cunningly concealed, and the forty survivors of the company reached the edge of the Grand Bois west of Cambron by nine o'clock. "D" company encountered similar resistance; but two platoons, though hindered by the difficulty of making their way through thick undergrowth, reached their objective a little later, and by eleven o'clock the company was in position for the next phase of the attack, with the remnant of "C" holding the northern front of the wood. The enemy, they reported, had no great strength in that vicinity, but his machine-gun posts were well sited, and "they naturally hamper the attack," said the Gordons apologetically.

They were eager to go on, however. They pressed for permission to advance on their second objective, but General Fortune had to refuse them. The centre had not kept pace with them, and their right flank was vulnerable. Even their first objective was untenable, and they were ordered to withdraw. The defeat of the French 31st Division, and the annihilation of its tanks, spelt failure for all; and the Abbeville bridgehead remained.

On the extreme left the 8th Argyll and Sutherlands—154th Brigade—had been cast for a quiet role in the day's action, but their Commanding Officer, Lieut.-Colonel Grant, had ideas of his own. He had suggested a local attempt to reduce the German bridgehead at St Valéry-sur-Somme; but the Division, under French command, was preoccupied with the Abbeville front, and Grant was disappointed. But with the help of Major Towers, R.A., commanding a battery of the 17th Field Regiment in St Blimont, he staged an interesting diversion. With an observation-post and a wireless-telephone truck at Le Hourdel, they shelled German machine-gun pits in the marshes west of the citadel of St Valéry, and Le Crotoy, across the river, where the enemy appeared to be concentrating. Though without immediate influence on the battle, the bombardment of Le Crotoy, at extreme range, had gratifying effects.

The 152nd Brigade lost twenty officers and five hundred and forty-three other ranks in the day's fighting. Its battalions had been exposed to close machine-gun fire, to mortars, artillery, and dive-bombing; and the Highlanders had not spared themselves. They had been signally unwilling to admit defeat, and when defeat could no longer be denied, they often retained a stubbornly independent attitude to it. Sergeant MacLeod, for instance, left wounded and alone on the Caubert ridge, eluded the enemy for two days and nights, and finally rejoined his battalion. David Ross, who had fought his way into the village of Caubert, was later reported missing; but on June 6th, forty-eight hours after the battle, he reappeared at Martaineville with another officer and sixty Cameron Highlanders whom he had led through ten or a dozen miles of country infested by the enemy's mobile forces. And Lieutenant Hugh Macrae, 4th Seaforths, who was wounded in the assault on the ridge but reached the farthest forward position, lay there till nightfall, and then of his two and half score men, all of whom were casualties, painfully sought and collected the few who could walk, and led them to the nearest Regimental Aid Post, saving them from certain capture.

6. The Germans Drive Forward

THE GERMANS, steadily reinforced, pushed their attack without delay, and it soon became apparent that the Division had no hope of holding its twenty-mile front against such forces as the enemy was able to concentrate. He renewed the battle at daybreak on the 5th, now thrusting most strongly against the 154th Brigade, which was thinly spread from Quesnoy to Le Hourdel and the sea: a front of eight miles or so. The 1st Black Watch had not returned from loan to the 153rd, and the 154th, with both battalions in the line, had no Brigade reserve.

The three villages of Saigneville, Mons and Catigny were held by the 7th Argyll and Sutherland Highlanders, and these were vigorously attacked by infantry-carriers, motor-borne machine-guns, and some armoured vehicles. On the left of the 7th, between Catigny and the sea, were the 8th Argylls; they too were heavily assailed.

"B" company of the 7th, with a machine-gun section of the Northumberland Fusiliers, repulsed a German attack on Saigneville, and directed artillery fire on a German concentration in a nearby ravine. At eight o'clock their telephone was cut, but they had sufficient peace and appetite to eat a quiet breakfast half an hour later. "C" company, at Mons, was surrounded soon after dawn by an estimated force of a thousand infantry, and "D" company at Catigny, having repelled an attack supported by light tanks, withdrew to St Blimont, which was held by a company of the 8th, leaving Second-Lieutenant Green—who had been with the battalion for one day only—to hold with his platoon the cross-roads at Arrest. Green was not heard of again.

Touch was then lost with these advanced companies, and Battalion Headquarters at Franleu were also surrounded.

The German stream, by now, was driving the Division back along its whole front. As the incoming tide, advancing over flattish sand, comes in by sudden trickles or runnels—a channel here, a channel there—then, drowning the islets it has surrounded, goes on with never-deviating purpose, though still by unexpected sallies, so the Germans found gaps and entry in the twenty miles of hill, hedgerow, village, wood and rolling field from Limeux to the sea. The front was too long, its defenders too few. It was a physical, a numerical impossibility to hold so long a line with only one division; but nowhere was it abandoned without fighting.

When the enemy by-passed or overran the forward companies of the 7th Argylls, the 1st Gordons on their right were left in an untenable salient between Saigneville and Gouy, with the Germans thrusting deeply past them towards Quesnoy. "A" company at Quesnoy was surrounded, and another company, going to its help from somewhere in front of Miannay, crossed a ridge and came under the fire of German mortars and infantry-guns. Some degree of control was restored, after fighting, and the Gordons were ordered to face left and occupy the high ground overlooking the railway from Cahon to Hymmeville.

On their right, between Lambercourt and Toeuffles, the 1st Black Watch was holding a front of two and a half miles. They were well placed in natural cover, with, in many places, a thousand yards of open country before them, and Private McCready—whose correspondence has already been quoted—describes their defence: "Cpl. Spalding was killed in this position, which was the best the Battalion had, he was killed by a sniper who was spotted by one of the A/T Detachment. Cpl. Spalding was soon avenged. We held these positions for two days, and hand-to-hand fighting took place in "D" company area. The enemy had to cross a river and advance up hill over open ground, they evidently had no idea of our position. 'C' Coy. held their fire until they were 200 yards away, then let them have it. I was reinforcing one of the A/T guns at that time, as Martin was badly shell-shocked and another A/T man was killed. 'D' Coy. fire was terrific, the enemy had no chance at all.

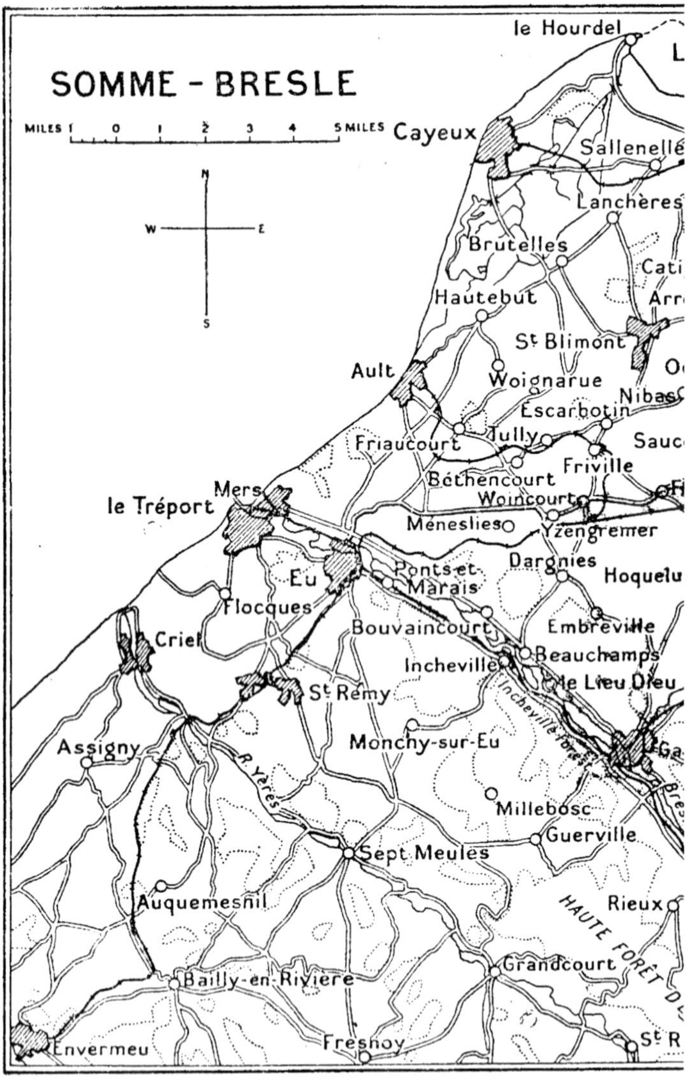

SOMME - BRESLE
MILES 1 0 1 2 3 4 5 MILES
N
W
E
S
le Hourdel
Cayeux
Sallenelle
Lanchères
Brutelles
Hautebut
St Blimont
Ault
Woignarue
Nibas
Escarbotin
Friaucourt
Tully
Friville
Béthencourt
Mers
le Tréport
Woincourt
Méneslies
Yzengremer
Dargnies
Hoquelu
Ponts-et-Marais
Eu
Flocques
Criel
Bouvaincourt
Embreville
Beauchamps
Incheville
le Lieu Dieu
St Rémy
Incheville forest
Monchy-sur-Eu
Assigny
R. Yères
Millebosc
Guerville
Sept Meules
Auquemesnil
HAUTE FORÊT D
Rieux
Grandcourt
Bailly-en-Rivière
Freshoy
Envermeu

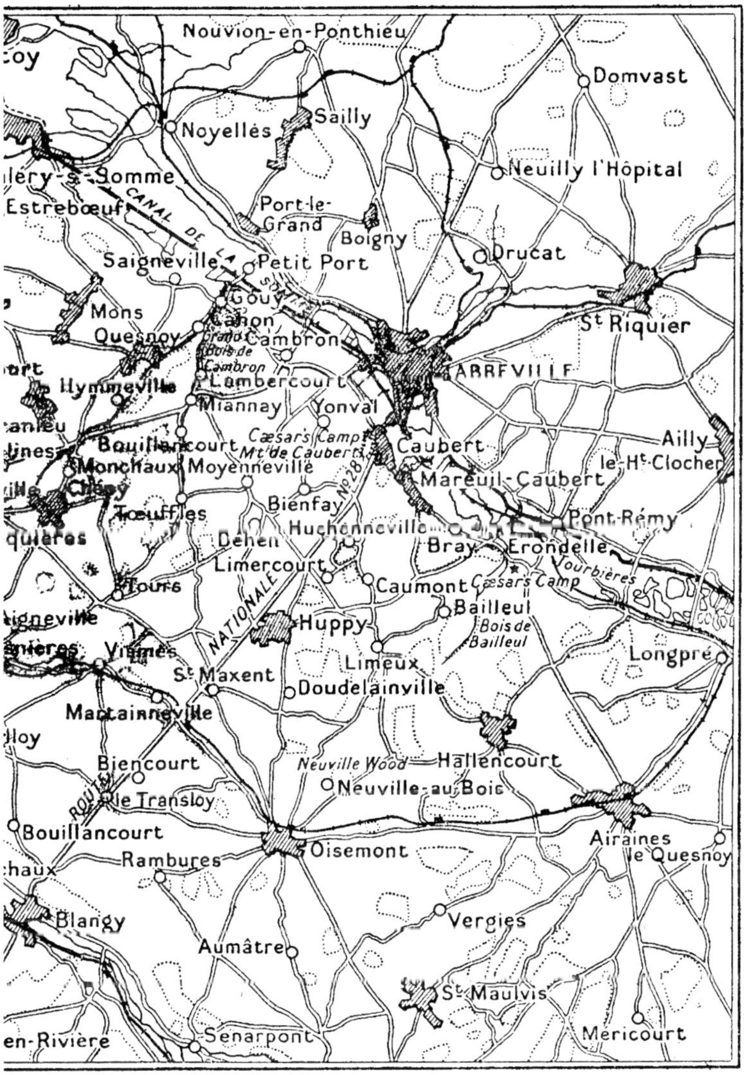

Nouvion-en-Ponthieu
Domvast
Sailly
Noyelles
Neuilly l'Hôpital
Estrebœuf
CANAL DE LA SOMME
Port-le-Grand
Boigny
Drucat
Saigneville
Petit Port
St Riquier
Mons
Gouy
Cahon
Quesnoy
Cambron
Grand Bois de Cambron
Hymmeville
Lambercourt
ABBEVILLE
Miannay
Yonval
Ailly
Bouillancourt
Cæsar's Camp
Mt de Caubert
Caubert
le Ht Clocher
Monchaux
Moyenneville
Mareuil-Caubert
Tœuffles
Bienfay
No 28
Pont-Rémy
Huchenneville
Behen
Bray
Erondelle
Limercourt
Yourbières
Tours
Caumont
Cæsar's Camp
Bailleul
Bois de Bailleul
NATIONALE
Huppy
Vismes
Limeux
Longpré
St Maxent
Doudelainville
Martainneville
Neuville Wood
Hallencourt
Biencourt
Neuville-au-Bois
ROUTE
le Transloy
Bouillancourt
Airaines
Oisemont
le Quesnoy
Rambures
Vergies
Blangy
Aumâtre
St Maulvis
Mericourt
Senarpont
en-Rivière

Nutting was badly wounded there in 5 different places, but he was very cheerful although he must have been suffering terribly. That same day Bn. H.Q. was shelled, the C.O.'s batman was killed, and the R.S.M. wounded in the hand. . . ."

The Germans were making full use of all their resources, including captured equipment. The Highlanders found it particularly galling to identify British machine-guns among the attackers' weapons, and to see the enemy using British staff-cars, their dun camouflage distinguished by a large W to show the Wehrmacht's ownership. But McCready is right in claiming for his battalion a day of notable execution in this area. The Germans, halted for a considerable time, suffered heavy losses not only from the Black Watch, but from the well-directed machine-gun fire of a French regiment between Bienfay and Moyenneville, and from artillery fire.

But eventually the company at Lambercourt was driven in, the line swung back on Toeuffles, and the new position was held till night.

Lothians in Action

On the right of the front, on the high ground to the right of Mareuil–Caubert, "A" squadron of the Lothians and Border Horse, in anticipation of a hard day, had fortified themselves with French poultry and their position with a French tank. The tank had broken down, but its crew were standing by, and its guns—a two-pounder and a machine-gun—were in working order. At a quarter-past four there was heavy firing on the right: the German attack had opened on "C" squadron, at Bray. "C" squadron was hard pressed, but with the aid of the carrier-troop from "A" rebuffed the offensive.

Then "A" squadron was surprised by the sudden appearance of German infantry. Two scouts came round a corner, and found themselves face to face with the

French tank. The leading scout halted and put up his hands. The second man shot him in the back. Then someone in "A" squadron shot the second man. After this spirited opening, the attack developed on more conventional lines: from an opposite ridge and from a flank overlooking the Somme there came mortar-bombs and machine-gun fire. But the French tank's two-pounder was very effective against the enemy's machine-guns, and the position was held till noon. But by then the tank had used all its ammunition, and the German artillery was registering with accuracy: the northern posts were therefore evacuated. Skirmishing continued till the late afternoon, when orders were received to withdraw if possible.

The squadron had for some time been out of touch with Regimental Headquarters, which by ten o'clock in the morning had, from the air, been blasted out of the Bois de Bailleul * and compelled to retire to Doudelainville. The attack of the dive-bombers had been fierce, and all ranks had discovered the use of a hole in the ground: the deeper and narrower the better. Then, following the Regiment, an officer from "A" squadron arrived with a report on the forward position, and returned with instructions to retire. To retire—a sinister addition—if possible. Major Dallmeyer, indeed, commanding "A" squadron, had considerable difficulty in extricating his men, and a hazardous march before him. But he rejoined the Regiment before midnight with some twenty-five men, having lost forty in the day's fighting. "C" squadron had returned some hours earlier.

The rearguard action began. Orders were given for withdrawal to immediate positions on the line Limeux–Limercourt–Moyenneville–Valines–Escarbotin–Hautebut. This line would be held, if possible, till half an hour before midnight of the 5th, and preparations would

* The place from which John Balliol, King of Scotland, took his name.

also be made to offer resistance on the line of the river Bresle.

The Germans had thrust hard against Valines, and their advance was most decisive along the coast. There, on our left front, the 8th Argylls had been driven back and lost touch with their two forward companies. "A" company, at Sallenelle, had been attacked by armoured vehicles and numerous infantry. When the enemy's patrols penetrated to the main street of the village—from which, but a little while before, a wounded despatch-rider had been evacuated in a perambulator—the survivors, seventy men out of a hundred and thirty, persisted in a confused sort of street-fighting. A number of them, lining a wall in front of Company Headquarters, exchanged grenades over the opposite buildings with Germans gathered on the other side. Though the situation was desperate, it was not, it appears, regarded as unduly serious; for when Lieutenant Paton, who had been wounded in the leg while on patrol the day before, threw a bomb which fell short, hit a roof and bounced back, there was fairly general hilarity, and his further throwing was handicapped by facetious cries of "Careful, George!"

When orders came to retire it was difficult to extricate the men from such close-quarter fighting, but orchards west of the village gave good cover, and most of them got out. They retired to Lanchères, then to Brutelles, where they met "B" company, and later to Hautebut. But there was no safety there, for by then our left wing had fallen back on the Ault–Tully–Friville line. The two companies were left behind.

Camerons Dive-bombed

Brigadier Stanley-Clarke, commanding the 154th Brigade, had by six o'clock withdrawn his headquarters to Dargnies, and the Brigade artillery had all gone back except two troops of the 17th Field Regiment caught at Ochancourt. The situation at dusk was summarised as follows: The 8th Argylls were believed to be holding the Ault–Tully–Escarbotin line, with the 7th Northumberland Fusiliers between Escarbotin and Fressenville, and the 4th Black Watch holding Fressenville to Feuquières. Contact had been lost with the 153rd Brigade on the right, and the enemy's forward elements were already between Dargnies and the Bresle. Some of the bridges over the Bresle had already been blown.

The 152nd Brigade, on the right, had fallen back to the railway line running north-west from Oisemont to the main road from Blangy to Abbeville. Their numbers gravely diminished in the battle for the bridgehead, and now tired by a long day's rearguard action, the men were too exhausted to stop a serious attack. In the afternoon, not far from Martaineville, about two hundred men of the 4th Camerons were retiring in extended order across deep fields of clover when they were attacked, three times in succession, by three dive-bombers. There was no cover but the clover. The men lay down. They were thankful for the rest, and most of them fell asleep. They suffered no casualties—three bullets through an empty water-bottle made the nearest miss—but once they had gone to ground, even dive-bombers could not keep the men awake.

The dive-bombers, indeed, though they made a most horrible and alarming din, caused curiously little damage to their legitimate targets. Against the civilian refugees, who made a heavy traffic all through these June days, they were more successful. They had a decided preference for refugees, among whom they did, with triumph, great feats of murder. But the troops, who had been taught to lie down, take cover where possible, and keep still, suffered little, and often had no more to complain about than the abominable noise.

It is hardly possible to give a complete and orderly picture of the day's fighting, but the nature of it is well illustrated by the following message—typical of many—received from a Company Commander of the 4th Black Watch: "Carriers in contact with enemy. Receiving casualties and state unable to contain enemy who are in large numbers. Consider we may be cut off on left. Any instructions?"

Gunner's Log

Flux and uncertainty, encirclement and escape, and the dogged defence of isolated localities like Franleu, characterised all that hot summer day. Its incessant movement, and the typical feature of deep enemy infiltration—made possible by the excessive length of the Divisional front—are shown very clearly in the following extract from the War Diary of the 17th Field Regiment, Royal Artillery :

5th June.

0425 hrs.	Right O.P. reports Boche patrol coming from Neuville wood.
0440 ,,	7th A. & S.H. report they are firing hard over their perimeter at Boches in direction Arrest.
0442 ,,	Right O.P. reports evacuation just in time.
0450 ,,	240th Med. Bty. surrounded and evacuated, taking locks of guns, escaping in tractors.
0500 ,,	Report from 10/26th Fd. Bty. that "A" troop wagon-lines surrounded and captured.
0510 ,,	"C" troop ordered up-sticks, go back to a hide. Officers and detachment of "C" troop sent up with rifles and Bren guns to help defend "A" troop gun positions, where firing at point-blank range.
0520 ,,	Situation reported to H.Q., R.A., 51st, with request for help.
0530 ,,	"A" troop reported surrounded and captured, and enemy advancing on Command Post.
0540 ,,	Message from the 154th Bde. that Bren-carriers of 8th A. & S.H. coming to help 10/26th Fd. Bty.

0600 hrs. Last communication with 7th A. & S.H. who report they are holding out in Franleu.

0615 „ Message sent with 2/Lt. Turner to get "C" troop into action about Fressenville.

0630 „ No sign of carriers of 8th A. & S.H. Orders to 13/92nd Fd. Bty. to send two armoured O.P.'s under 2/Lt. Fisher to Ochancourt, to help 10/26th Fd. Bty. These got as far as Nibas and did excellent work for 2½ hrs., holding the enemy till relieved by carriers of 8th A. & S.H. Mortar reported shelling Ochancourt church.

0700 „ Last communication received from 10/26th Fd. Bty.—"Cheerio, coming to join you."

0810 „ Orders given that in case of withdrawal all batteries would come into action south of River Bresle, with H.Q. at Monchy.

0820 „ Orders given to all batteries for withdrawal parties to proceed to cross-roads Beauchamps.

0830 „ Enemy M.T. reported at 625914. Engaged by 13/92nd Fd. Bty. News that remnants of 10/26th Fd. Bty. from Ochancourt have reached Nibas. . . .

All this before breakfast-time. And while this was going on, while the gunners were reconnoitring their possible withdrawal to the Bresle, and there was fighting round Ochancourt and Nibas and Franleu, "B" company of the 7th Argylls, in Saigneville, half a dozen miles to the east of Nibas, were indeed eating their breakfast in comparative peace. The Germans had gone on, and left them behind.

The War Diary continues:

0923 hrs. "B" troop, 240th Med. Bty., reports that position is none too secure, but no undue cause for alarm.

0946 „ "B" troop, 240th Med. Bty., still in action and firing continuously at rapid rate.

0950 „ 13/92nd Fd. Bty. report they are firing incessantly at rapid rate.

0952 „ "B" troop, 240th Med. Bty., report enemy 700 yds. away on left. . . .

Ten minutes later "B" troop reported that the infantry were retreating through them, and the enemy steadily advancing. They were ordered to withdraw. Regimental Headquarters closed down and withdrew to the rendezvous at Beauchamps.

To their right, in the centre of the line, the guns of the 75th Field Regiment—Territorials from Aberdeen—had had similar narrow escapes. On open ground they had dealt heavy blows to the Germans, but despite their losses the Germans still came on. Two guns in "E" troop fired over eight hundred and fifty shells each during the day, and before it was over some of the gunners were unconscious under the strain of continuous noise and fatigue.

7. The Fight at Franleu

THE VILLAGE of Franleu became the scene of a very stubborn, heroic conflict.

At daybreak, or soon after, a sergeant riding a motor-bicycle left Franleu to repair a telephone line. He was shot. The Regimental Sergeant-Major of the 7th Argylls went out with three men and found the Germans, in large numbers, astride the road from Arrest. The defence of the village was swiftly organised, Bren guns removed from half a dozen carriers for use in section-posts, and a patrol set out to deal with snipers. Then the telephone line to Brigade Headquarters was cut, but a subaltern, though shot at by Germans, in the southern parts of the village, got through to Hoquelus and reported the situation.

At five o'clock Lieut.-Colonel Buchanan, commanding the 7th Argylls, ordered "A" company, holding the village of Quesnoy, to withdraw to Franleu to assist in its defence. No Germans had as yet been seen at Quesnoy, and "A" company at once put its Bren gunners and their guns into the cooks' lorry and sent them off. The Company Commander followed in a utility truck, and the remainder marched. The Company Commander, getting out to reconnoitre the cross-roads north-east of Franleu, was shot in the back by a sniper.

"A" company was disposed right and left of Battalion Headquarters, which were situated in the village school, some little distance from the village itself. Bren gunners lined the nearby hedges, and the defenders' only mortar did good work. But the Germans had five-inch mortars, heavy weapons of great accuracy, and they were far superior in numbers. More of their lorry-borne infantry arrived, and four more mortars, horse-drawn, came into position. Their fire grew more intense, but they showed no inclination to come into the open.

Water and chocolate were sent to the men outside. The only carrier that was still armed, under Lance-Corporal Currie, patrolled the streets, dealt with snipers, and brought in wounded. The school had a cellar, which became a dressing-station, and there the Chaplain, the Rev. Duncan McInnes, tended the growing number of wounded.

Brigadier Stanley-Clarke obtained from Divisional reserve the 4th Black Watch and ten French tanks, and sent them to the relief of Franleu.

But neither tanks nor infantry could make headway against the stream of Germans flooding south-west. By two o'clock in the afternoon the leading company of the Black Watch had already found Germans on the railway-line north of Feuquières. "B" and "D" companies were nominated for the relief, and the troop of light tanks available to support them was commanded by a French officer who was not only prepared but eager to attack. Before they were ready to go forward, however, the enemy was pouring down the road from Abbeville to

Eu, and Saucourt—a village half-way between Feuquières and Franleu—was apparently held in strength. The tanks and a platoon of "D" company harassed the Germans in Saucourt, but the relief of Franleu was held to be impossible, and the attack was abandoned.

Through the Besiegers' Ring

Franleu, in the meantime, was still holding on. The only mortar had done valiantly against the many German weapons, and the enemy had twice been driven back when, extended in double line, under cover of smoke they had tried to rush the village. But the German bombardment had done great damage, and there were many wounded in the cellar below the village school. A machine-gun section of the Northumberland Fusiliers had been particularly successful, but early in the afternoon it was silenced. And a little later in the afternoon the solitary invaluable mortar was put out of action by a direct hit. In the growing heat of afternoon—summer's heat and the heat of burning houses—German reinforcements arrived—three tanks, motor-cycle troops, four hundred infantry. But still the enemy was held away, though no help came for the small and weary garrison.

Then, about five o'clock, a mortar-bomb hit the last remaining ammunition-truck, which took fire and blew up, and made a wreck of Battalion Headquarters. Captain Robertson, who had organised the defence, was wounded, and so were Major Younger, Regimental Sergeant-Major Lockie, Company Sergeant-Major Dyer; they had, throughout the day, shown tireless energy and set for all a magnificent example. In the section-posts, in houses and on the outskirts of the village, there were by now many wounded men and many dead. There was no reserve of ammunition, no hope of reinforcement. An hour after the blowing-up of the ammunition-truck, Colonel Buchanan took stock and decided that the defence could not be maintained. He was unable to communicate with some of the outlying sections; but the others were told to use what vehicles they could find, and try to break through the German lines.

By ditch and hedge the Colonel led his survivors to the farm buildings a hundred yards away, where transport had been parked. Three or four trucks crammed with men, of whom many were wounded, and two carriers ran the gauntlet. They got through. They were hotly fired on as they broke out of Franleu, but once through the besieging ring and they were almost safe. For every German gun was pointed inwards, against the village.

While the trucks were being loaded the Colonel's batman, Allan Carswell, his left sleeve hanging bloodily by his side, came to ask the Colonel for the loan of his revolver. "What do you want it for?" asked the Colonel. "Can you not see that I've got a broken arm? I can't use a rifle," said Carswell. He was a quiet, shy man who had been a forester; but now, with his revolver and his one good arm, he set off on his solitary counter-attack, while the Colonel went back to the cellar under Battalion Headquarters, where there were about thirty badly wounded men. Before the others left, two volunteers had been asked to stay with them. Volunteers had immediately offered. The padre, the Rev. Duncan McInnes, also elected to remain. Throughout the day he had cared for the wounded with unceasing devotion, and when the German snipers were shooting with great accuracy into the precincts of the school, he had gone out against their fire to fetch water for his patients. Now, on all sides, there were buildings aflame, and though the last of its defenders had gone, the Germans were still lobbing their mortar-bombs into Franleu.

By the end of the day twenty-three officers and some five hundred other ranks of the 7th Argyll and Sutherland Highlanders were killed, wounded, or missing.

8. Fight and March and Fight Again

AT DAWN on June 6th, the Division, with certain French troops between the centre and right Brigades, was extended along a line from Oisemont, through Vismes and Fressenville, to Friaucourt or thereabout. There was, however, no hope of holding this line. The Division had orders to delay the German advance beyond it for a limited period only. Withdrawal across the Bresle was already decided, and the new front would run from Blangy to the sea. The French 31st Division, side-stepping to the east, was removing from the area. Eastward of the Somme the French were now on the line of the river Aisne.

The Friaucourt–Oisemont line was never water-tight: there was considerable German leakage in the neighbourhood of Dargnies, where were the Headquarters of the 154th Brigade; and an anti-tank battery which, during the night of June 5th, had been ordered to retire from the vicinity of Saucourt across the Bresle, had been fired on by German mortars on the east bank of the river in the vicinity of Ponts-et-Marais. In the early hours of the 6th the remnants of "D" company of the 7th Argyll and Sutherlands had exchanged grenades with the enemy at Woincourt, and then retired to Dargnies. There it was heavily mortared, and withdrawing to Fucheville on the Bresle, held the bridge with the Headquarters Company of the 8th Argylls, which at daybreak had been in Yzengrèmer.

A squadron of tanks had gone from Dargnies to Yzengrèmer in the early morning. Reconnoitring forward, the tanks found a number of German machine-gun posts, and went to look for roads of approach and attack; but without success. Mortar-fire, moving from north to north-west, grew heavier on the Argylls' position, and was aggravated by machine-guns. The

Argylls had nothing better than Bren guns with which to reply, and had to fall back on Dargnies. There it was learnt that light mechanised forces of the enemy were already in Eu.

The tanks brought thirty-five prisoners into Dargnies, and returned to hold the railway-line south of Yzengrèmer. The 4th Black Watch, ordered to withdraw from Friville and Fressenville, occupied a line from Dargnies to Hoquelus, and the 153rd Brigade still maintained its Headquarters at Aigneville. On the extreme left of the 154th Brigade front there was no defence but some posts on the river Bresle held by the Pioneer battalion of the Royal Scots Fusiliers.

"B" echelon of the 7th Argylls, with the survivors of Franleu, had been ordered across the Bresle to the Incheville Forest and thence to St Rémy. But in St Rémy it was reported that German tanks had broken through in the neighbourhood of Incheville, and the Argylls went back to a position in the forest.

The pretence of holding, even for a day, an intermediate line between the Somme and the Bresle had to be abandoned. We had neither enough troops nor sufficient fire-power to meet the enemy's attack, the main stream of which was now flowing against our coastal flank. The Germans could no more be contained than water in a basket; our line, torn open on the left, was as full of holes as wattle, and there were no adequate reserves with which to close them. It had become perfectly clear that General Fortune could hope for nothing better than a rearguard action, by which he might punish and delay the German advance, maintain the cohesion of the Division, and keep touch with the French formations that were falling back on his right.

From Dargnies and Hoquelus the 4th Black Watch, under cover of fire from a company of the 1st Gordons, retired to new positions overlooking Beauchamps. They had been heavily shelled, they had no food, the men were nearly exhausted. By now, indeed, the whole Division was feeling the effect of its long period of almost incessant movement, of battle and march and battle again, with little time for sleep and none to recuperate and reorganise. To the east of Gamaches the 1st Black Watch were for a little while remote from the enemy's ground forces, so they "slept for a few hours, being bombed and machine-gunned from the air, but suffered no casualties, and all were much too tired to mind."

Oisemont was attacked by the Germans in the early afternoon. French motor-cyclist machine-gunners shared the defence with the Lothians and did well. The attack was reinforced from the air, a petrol storage tank was set ablaze, and the flames spread through the village. The position was held till nine at night, when the Lothians withdrew, and, crossing the Bresle at Blangy, found harbour in the western end of the Haute Forêt d'Eu.

A Bottle and a Bridge

Three nights before, the Route Nationale north-east of Blangy had been thickly crowded with the troops and ammunition-trucks of the 31st French Division. Now, for long intervals, it was empty as a desert. Darkness descended upon the village of Biencourt, and Lord Cawdor, commanding the 4th Camerons, sent back his last section of carriers. No other transport remained in the village, so he and his French liaison officer had to walk. Except for themselves the road was empty. But for the noise of their boots on its hard surface, the night was altogether silent. In this desolated quietness they walked to Le Transloy, and there at the cross-roads they found a military policeman. There were still some troops on the enemy's side of the Bresle, and the Red-cap was calmly waiting to direct this remaining traffic.

They waited together, and presently there appeared

a platoon of the 4th Seaforths, and then the remains of a company of the 4th Camerons from the Oisemont railway-line. Then, some time after one o'clock, they came to Blangy, where a Sapper officer was waiting to blow the bridge at two. But the demolition was postponed till four o'clock, to give any stragglers a chance to cross.

The night was hot, and there was an estaminet at the bridge. It had been abandoned, and the door was locked. But the cutting-charge under the bridge was very heavy, said the Sapper, and would certainly destroy the estaminet as well. To break open the door would merely be anticipation of the inevitable. So they entered and fortunately discovered a bottle or two of Châteauneuf du Pape, which they drank sitting on the parapet of the bridge. Then, at four in the morning, when it was near daylight, the Sapper pressed a button, and bridge and estaminet collapsed together.

West of Blangy in the Haute Forêt was the 51st Medium Regiment, Royal Artillery. During the afternoon of the 6th it had been in action against the German left. Then orders came to shell Ponts-et-Marais, and to engage this target the guns of the 215th troop had to be manhandled and swung round 120 degrees. Maps were scarce. The troop had one only, which was very crumpled and showed no contours. But line and range were measured on it, the angle of sight was guessed, a hundred yards was added for the meteorological factor—or for luck—and the new line transferred to the gun from a director seventy-five yards away. . . . An O.P. reported that the shelling was most effective.

In front of Gamaches, which was burning fiercely in places, there was typical uncertainty about the enemy's movement. The 1st Gordons were about to cross the river, but the Commanding Officer had some reason to fear that the Germans had broken through on his left, and might reach the bridge before him. Then he made contact with the 75th Field Regiment, who in the early afternoon had found themselves short of ammunition, and were also withdrawing. Some of their guns were retiring through Gamaches, and the Colonel of the Gordons arranged with them to cover the infantry's withdrawal from a position three hundred yards south of the bridge.

At nightfall the 4th Black Watch crossed the river at Beauchamps after holding a position in front of the bridge, enduring a heavy bombardment there, and suffering a good many casualties. Their new positions skirted the Incheville Forest, to which the enemy had already penetrated and where his menace was obviously dangerous. The 154th Brigade, after fighting all day on its eight-mile line, was reduced to less than fifty per cent. of its effective strength. A new Brigade had been brought up to its support, thanks to the fact that the Highland Division was still in touch with the lines of communication originally established for the main B.E.F. The battalions of this new Brigade had been working independently of each other on the lines of communication. They had never served together as a formation, and had had no Brigade training. Thus, though essentially fine troops, the formation was in some degree improvised. It was named "A" Brigade, and was composed of the 4th Battalion Buffs, the 4th Battalion Border Regiment, and the 5th Battalion Sherwood Foresters. It now lay south of the Bresle, facing the Forêt d'Incheville.

A Nest of Wrathful Englishmen

The defensive scheme on the morning of June 7th exhibited five sectors. On the right, from Blangy to Monchaux, was the 152nd Brigade. Left of them, to Gamaches, was the 153rd. To their left, as far as Beauchamps, the 154th Brigade. From Beauchamps to Eu was "A" Brigade, and from Eu to the sea the 6th Royal Scots Fusiliers.

That was the position on paper. But the 152nd Brigade had been so grossly mutilated in the last two days of fighting that what was left of it was presently withdrawn into reserve in the Haute Forêt, and its sector was taken over by the French. There was, too, some confusion on the left, for "A" Brigade, arriving in rather precipitous fashion, had occupied certain positions that properly belonged to the 154th. And in this area there were appreciable numbers of the enemy, who had crossed the river at Beauchamps.

The immediate task was to close the exits from the Incheville Forest, and eliminate its German occupants. This was "A" Brigade's duty, and initially it made progress. It was reported, indeed, that the counter-attack had been successful, and "A" Brigade had made good the line of the Bresle. But in spite of artillery support, the forest was not easy to clear. The 4th Battalion of the Border Regiment made the most strenuous and gallant efforts to dislodge the enemy, and Lieut.-Colonel Tomlinson, commanding the Battalion, handled his companies with great daring and imaginative energy. It was found at one time that his Headquarters Company was in action with the others, and he had no reserve whatsoever. He was given a company of the Sherwood Foresters—and very soon they also were in the battle. If the Germans could not be destroyed, they must at any cost be prevented from filtering to the south and turning the whole line. Tomlinson, moving his companies here and there, infecting his men with his own courageous enthusiasm, for two days sustained this vital responsibility, and with his half-trained Territorials pinned the enemy to a harmless corner of the forest. When at last the Battalion was ordered to withdraw, one of the companies, surrounded near the river bank, could not be extricated. It remained, and continued to fight. Beyond all hope of relief it went on fighting, and five days later there was still a nest of wrathful, indomitable Englishmen maintaining their cause in the Incheville wood. . . .

To the right of "A" Brigade was the 4th Black Watch, with a composite company made of the remnants of the two Argyll and Sutherland battalions and the 26th Field Company, Royal Engineers, and east along the Bresle from them, towards Gamaches, were the 1st Gordons.

Throughout the day the artillery was active on both sides. From an observation post overlooking Incheville the German columns could be seen advancing, a steady stream, from the direction of Dargnies, and concentrating on Beauchamps. Our twenty-five-pounders shelled them there, but could not stop their progress. The 51st Medium Regiment, with only six guns serviceable, did some admirable shooting from the neighbourhood of Millebosc. The 4th Black Watch suffered considerably from the enemy's fire, but held their front, and all day the enemy—except for minor infiltration and the break at Incheville—was confined to his own side of the river.

Unfortunately, however, there was very little to restrain the Luftwaffe's activity, despite the assistance of some of our fighter aircraft, and the Division had to endure again the repeated attack of dive-bombers.

The Royal Air Force could only give Fighter support to the battle in Normandy from the few aerodromes which had been hurriedly prepared. Fighter squadrons flew over from England for the day's work and returned at night. For the most part, these Fighters went into action over the French portion of the front, where the tactical situation was even more critical and the Highland Division had to suffer. Bomber squadrons based in England were continually attacking targets on the German communications. These attacks were out of sight of the fighting troops in the line, who almost always find it difficult to weigh the effect of such air action on the general course of a battle.

In the early morning of June 7th a reinforcement of nine hundred men had arrived from Rouen, a welcome aid; but in the evening disastrous tidings came from there. The enemy's armoured divisions had broken through the French at Amiens, and were advancing on the axis Amiens–Poix–Rouen. The French IX Corps was being torn apart from the rest of the Xth Army, to which it belonged; and the Fifty-First would be cut off from Rouen, which was its base of supply.

Hurried arrangements were made to use Le Havre as an alternative source of fuel and ammunition. It would mean long journeys for the R.A.S.C. echelon, but the handicap must be accepted. There was, however, no gun ammunition available at Le Havre, so a last train was loaded at Rouen, with shell and anti-tank mines, and sent from there to be left *en cas mobile* in the neighbourhood of Foucart. But it never arrived. It was searched for and could not be found. The Germans must have intercepted and captured it somewhere between Clères and Bolbec.

9. Exploit of the Argylls

THE LINE of the Bresle was held till the evening of June 8th, and that day broke with a pleasant surprise: somewhat reduced in strength, "A" and "B" companies of the Argyll and Sutherland Highlanders, who had been cut off at Ault, rejoined their Brigade. . . .

About four o'clock on the afternoon of June 5th, Major Lorne Campbell had gone to withdraw the two companies from their exposed positions in Brutelles and Hautebut. His mission was somewhat retarded by four German tanks, and when at last he led "A" company into the village of Woignarue, they found a German soldier directing traffic and a continuous stream of enemy transport passing through.

They were fired on. They examined the possibility of attacking the village, but decided that a more useful move would be to occupy the villages of Ault and Friaucourt, and so prevent any further German penetration to the south. But the Germans, unfortunately, had already gone through Friaucourt, and the two companies were completely cut off.

On a cliff overlooking the village of Ault there is a lighthouse with neighbouring buildings, and a nearby school. Major Campbell decided to occupy and hold this commanding area, and found there, already in residence, a platoon of the 6th Royal Scots Fusiliers and fifteen French Marines with a 75-millimetre gun. It was, however, not a very good gun: it broke the first time it was fired. The defence was organised and when evening came the defence could see, on the road to Eu, a stream of traffic, and throughout the night they heard the noise of its continuing flow.

Taking a sanguine view of the battle that was going on, the lost garrison expected an Allied counter-attack which, from their advanced position, they would be able to help. But on the 6th they heard the sound of fighting grow fainter as it withdrew to the south-east, and of the counter-attack no hope could be discerned. The Germans ignored them, and the garrison resented this unprofitable state of peace: Campbell and the two Company Commanders agreed that they should try to get back to the Division.

In the afternoon they were somewhat worried by snipers, and took a couple of prisoners. At eight o'clock, when Campbell was detailing orders for the move, the Germans attacked with tanks that took station some distance away and bombarded the buildings with small quick-firing cannon using tracer shells. The building which the French Marines were holding was set on fire, and they surrendered. Half a dozen aeroplanes gave a demonstration of dive-bombing, but without bombs. The tank attack was not pressed, and presently concluded. The air attack appeared to be a skirmish in the war of nerves rather than a serious assault.

The Garrison Marched Out

The Jocks were delighted to hear of the promised sortie; preparations were quickly made, and transport destroyed. The garrison moved out at a quarter to twelve, taking with them their unwounded prisoner. The march was led by three fighting patrols, each commanded by an officer, and carrying wire-cutters to open gaps in all fences. If the columns were fired on, they would continue to march. If forced to a halt, they had a plan for all-round defence and would fight to a finish. If they were scattered, then *sauve qui peut*. Wounded, if they could not walk, must be left behind.

They marched on a compass-bearing, taking right angles to it for measured distances to avoid villages, and returning to the bearing. Their dawn objective was a wood at Bouvaincourt; but the German tank demonstration had delayed their start, and when daylight came they were west of the village of Méneslies. It was hard to find good cover. They tried an orchard, then a field of wheat. A German plane came over the wheat and quartered it like a hen-harrier. They moved to a hillside of whins and lay there all day in windless hot weather, with very little to eat or drink and nothing to do but keep still. They saw German motor-cyclist patrols, and German officers searching the countryside with glasses. But anywhere behind the actual battle zone, it appeared, the Germans were still thin on the ground.

In the morning they could hear firing from the direction

of Tully, to the north, but that died down about noon. They had no idea where the nearest British troops were, and decided to make for one of the crossings of the Bresle, seize it, and find out who was on the other side. Gamaches was too big: Le Lieu Dieu was a better prospect. The route was decided, and the compass-bearings, to clear Dargnies and Embreville.

At eleven o'clock they left the whins, and when crossing the Beauchamps road were fired on by an enemy sentry-group from a distance of about twenty yards. After some hesitation, they went on. The Germans ran off, but turned to fire again a few seconds later. The Argylls had come close to a battery position: they could see the aiming lamps, and then saw them hurriedly put out. The alarm was given. A reconnaissance plane came searching for them, circling the darkness overhead, and parachute flares were fired from every village for miles around. From Dargnies shots were fired at them, and at Embreville they had to wait for a confused column of German vehicles moving across their line of march. A motor-cyclist gave them a little trouble, and then they found themselves not far from a German battery that British guns were shelling.

One More River . . .

It was getting light, but there was no use stopping, and they climbed the ridge north-east of the Bresle. Just as they reached the top they were challenged from all round with shouts of "Hallo!"—French troops? It was quite possible. They halted, and Campbell shouted, "Etes vous Français?" He was answered in German, so they marched on and were half-way over before the enemy opened fire with machine-guns. The Germans, who were not very numerous, had been taken by surprise and did not fire much. The Argylls were soon over the ridge with no one hurt.

Le Lieu Dieu lay below them. A rearguard was left under the imperturbable Captain Webb, and "B" company formed for an attack. The village was reconnoitred, and it became apparent that the Argylls had come into No Man's Land. The morning mist lay in the valley. They hurried on and crossed the channels of the Bresle by the wreckage of two blown bridges, then waded a third stream. A rear party covered each crossing. Now their only danger was of being shot by their own side, but Second-Lieutenant Mackinnon with his patrol went forward at some risk, and the first man he saw was a private of the Black Watch carrying a pail and looking for a cow to milk. The Argylls had found their own Brigade and at least a temporary safety.

About the same time a diminutive gunner rejoined. Very young, short and slight, he had been taken prisoner at Béthencourt. A German officer, with some mercy and a small humour, told him he was too little to kill, but threatening him with a revolver, ordered him to stay where he was or he would be shot. Then he went off. The gunner waited for a while, but presently made friends with some French refugees, and when night came changed his uniform for civilian clothes. He pretended to be deaf and dumb, and came into our lines holding the hand of an old woman. The refugees were examined, and a sergeant-major who had searched the boy, and no doubt felt sorry for his infirmity, shouted to him in a kindly way, "Voulez-vous une bicyclette?" "I don't want a bloody bicycle," said the refugee. "I want to see an officer!"

10. Rumour and Retreat

DURING MOST of the day—the 8th—our artillery was active, and so was the German Air Force. The enemy's mortars—ubiquitous, innumerably reinforced, magnificently handled—continued to do damage, and Bren-carriers hunted his patrols in the Incheville woods. South-east of Incheville the 4th Black Watch were feeling the strain of unceasing German pressure, and from the extreme right of the front came the news that inland the situation grew worse and worse, where the French, like the Stock Exchange at Budget time, were a prey to rumours.

Not that rumours were necessary to create despondency and alarm: the truth was bad enough. Two Panzer divisions, the 5th and 7th, were already at Buchy, fifteen miles north-east of Rouen. With German tanks thirty miles behind it, there was no longer any hope of holding the line of the Bresle. There was no longer any purpose in fighting to deny the enemy every rood and furlong of the ground. There was no chance, for the Fifty-First, or any of the French IXth Corps, of a retirement east of Rouen. The only way of continued retreat was over the Seine west of Rouen, where some motor barges had been collected and the regular ferries warned of what they might have to do. But the utmost speed would be necessary if they were to reach the Seine. To avoid encirclement the slow rearguard action must become a swift and decisive withdrawal.

From the French IXth Corps orders came to retire to the general line of the Béthune. In the late afternoon there was a conference of Sector Commanders at St Rémy, where detailed instructions were issued. The Division was to use all its available R.A.S.C. vehicles as troop-carriers. If every truck did a double journey, the whole Division could be motor-borne. But each round trip would be about twenty-eight miles, and the roads were still crowded with human wreckage, with fugitives and burdened carts and broken motor-cars. The arteries of France were choked, and she was visibly dying. Audibly dying too, for dogs tied to the doors of deserted houses howled of starvation and cows unmilked in the fields bellowed with the agony of their bursting udders.

Withdrawal of the infantry from their forward positions was in some places a delicate process; but the Germans, with their dislike of nocturnal adventure, did not interfere, and from eleven at night till four in the morning the successive battalions were embussed and driven down the dark and crowded roads to their new lines. There had been no time to reconnoitre, and positions were not finally occupied till well after daybreak.

The 153rd Brigade and "A" Brigade, with the 75th and 17th Field Regiments and the 1st Royal Horse Artillery, were disposed along the river Eaulne from Envermeu to Ancourt, and thence northward to the coast at Belleville. The 154th Brigade was on the Varenne, from Martigny to Arques-la-Bataille; and the 152nd Brigade with the 23rd Field Regiment held the river from Arques to Dieppe. The 31st Division of the French IXth Corps, withdrawing with the Fifty-First, was responsible for the line of the Eaulne from Envermeu to the south-east.

The troops, tired though they were, set to work on defensive positions; but the Germans did not closely follow the withdrawal. The Lothians and Border Horse, covering the left flank of the withdrawal, were still in touch with the enemy, but to the rest of the Division the day brought no fighting.

During the morning of the 9th, officers of the Royal Navy arrived at Divisional Headquarters, at the château of La Chaussée, to discuss evacuation from Havre, where it was estimated that 23,000 men of the Fifty-First would require to be embarked. All arrangements had been made for this at Portsmouth and nine destroyers with a number of transports assembled off Havre that night (June 9th) ready for the task. The plight of the French and their Highland allies had become as desperate as that. The

German penetration towards Rouen would certainly be exploited—and swiftly exploited—and the prevailing belief was that the enemy would spread westward along the north bank of the Seine, to cut the IXth Corps' retreat and pen it against the sea. There was, perhaps, a danger even more imminent: when the last ammunition-train from Rouen failed to arrive at Foucart, and could nowhere be found, the Divisional Ammunition Company sent trucks to a dump in the forest of St Saëns—and found the forest on fire, the ammunition dumps exploding. If the enemy were at St Saëns in any strength, they might swing from there northward to the Channel: in that case, the only port from which the Allied Forces could hope to be evacuated was Dieppe. But in view of the rapid approach of the enemy, blocking vessels were on their way to that port, and the entrance was in fact blocked at dawn on June 10th just before the entry of the enemy. Twenty miles west of it was a small fishing harbour, St Valéry-en-Caux, drying at low water, and difficult both to find and to enter. According to naval opinion, the only practicable port for embarkation was Havre which, therefore, would have to be defended against the presumptive German advance from Rouen.

11. Ark Force

AT FOUR O'CLOCK in the afternoon, Brigadier Stanley-Clarke was instructed to undertake the defence of Le Havre with a force composed of the Headquarters of his own Brigade, the remnants of the two Argyll and Sutherland battalions, the 4th Black Watch, the 6th Royal Scots Fusiliers, Royal Artillery, Sappers, and the scratch group known as "A" Brigade.* This command was created in the village of Arques-la-Bataille, that lies

* See Order of Battle.

beside the ruins of a castle built by an uncle of William the Conqueror, which William undutifully besieged and captured, and after its birthplace it was christened Ark Force.

It was a memorable christening. The evening flight of German bombers was drumming through the clear sky towards Le Havre, and sitting on the warm summer turf, the senior officers of the Division heard General Fortune relate his plans and their growing danger. He had sent, he said, a personal appeal to the Prime Minister for all the air support that England could spare. The Navy was ready to do everything in its power to embark the Division and their Allies, but no one could promise a safe conclusion of their efforts. The Germans might strike north, between them and their goal. Fortune said nothing to smooth or lessen the perils of their situation, but he affirmed his confidence in success, and wished them good luck. This was also the day on which Weygand made elsewhere his cryptic statement: "Nous sommes au dernier quart d'heure. Tenez bon."

Ark Force was ordered to proceed that night to a position reaching from Fécamp to Lillebonne. From this line it would cover (such was the intention) the withdrawal to Le Havre of the remainder of the Division and the French IXth Corps. According to the French General's *directives*, the period of withdrawal would be three nights —it was considered inadvisable to move by day—and evacuation would not begin before June 13th.

The danger of so leisurely a plan must have been apparent to all, and was certainly obvious to General Fortune, who initially proposed a much faster retirement; but the French were unable to move with any speed. The greater part of their forces was marching infantry, and much of their transport was horse-drawn. The Fifty-First had sufficient motor vehicles to carry, if necessary, every man in the Division; if Fortune were to admit no responsibility but the safety of his own men he could very speedily arrive in Le Havre. But to retire at his own pace would expose the left flank of the French 31st Division. Loyalty had a greater claim than self-interest; and Fortune, accepting the burden that loyalty put upon him, ordered his withdrawal according to the French time-table.

Under a Ceiling of Smoke

The night of the 9th was preternaturally dark. Oil refineries at Le Havre and along the river Seine had been bombed and set on fire, and a great ceiling of black smoke, greasy and impenetrable, was spreading to the north-east. Even when daylight came above the smoke, the country beneath it lay for hours in a dun twilight, and the monstrous cloud, stretching more thinly over the Channel, covered the sea with a sullen fog. At night the transport drivers on the coast-road to Fécamp had to navigate a darkness so thick and evil-smelling as almost to be palpable. The roads, as they were at all times, were clotted with refugees, and French batteries were also on the move. Ark Force fumbled its way between gross but invisible obstacles, and struggled through black confusion to its goal.

By ten o'clock on the following morning a number of units had not yet reached Fécamp, and if the French intelligence reports were true, the Germans were already in its neighbourhood. The enemy was said to be within a few miles of Fécamp, within a few miles of Bolbec. And shortly after midday, Major C. P. R. Johnston arrived at Ark Force Headquarters with the news that the Fifty-First now appeared to be cut off from Le Havre. The General's instructions were that Brigadier Stanley-Clarke must, in these new circumstances, use his own judgment when selecting a defensive line. Ark Force might no longer be required to cover the Allied withdrawal.

There had been no time to make detailed reconnaissance of the Fécamp–Lillebonne line, but a much shorter line from Octeville to Montivilliers and thence south to Gonserville—enclosing the mere tip of the nose of the debatable land—had previously been reconnoitred by garrison troops in Le Havre. To meet the new and alarming situation it was hurriedly decided to hold the forward line between Lillebonne and Goderville with "A" Brigade, supported by the 17th Field Regiment, R.A., and a company of machine-gunners, in conjunction with certain French fixed posts between Lillebonne and Fécamp; and to concentrate on the inner line the remnants of the 154th Brigade, supported by the 75th Field Regiment and the remaining machine-gun company.

All that was left of the 154th Brigade withdrew during the 10th to the inner position, but the disposal of "A" Brigade on the Lillebonne–Goderville line was less accurately known. Its situation-reports were fragmentary, and news of it was difficult to obtain. It was learnt subsequently that the Buffs, arriving very late at Fécamp, had found Germans on the high ground east of the town, and in action against them had suffered severely. The 17th Field Regiment of Royal Artillery, surviving the confusion in Fécamp, took up a position between Lillebonne and Bréaute with no infantry to support it, and disposed its guns in an anti-tank role to guard approaches from the east.

12. Fate was in a Hurry

AT HALF-PAST three on the same morning, June 10th—the day of Italy's bold entry into the war—the 1st Black Watch, retiring from the Forêt d'Arques, occupied a position on the river Varenne with their left at Martigny. The men were so tired that they slept on their feet. Since May 30th they had, without rest, been fighting or marching or digging, they had rarely been out of range of field-gun or machine-gun, mortar or dive-bomber, and now if they halted for a few minutes they fell to the grass in a sleep so profound that boot and fist were needed to waken them. But somewhere within their dreadful weariness lay a reserve of strength, a fount of valour that was to carry them through another day, and yet another.

The first attack on their new position came from German infantry who, advancing behind a screen of refugees, opened fire from four hundred yards range on "B" Company Headquarters. By early afternoon the whole position was being shelled or mortar-bombed, and the forward companies were closely engaged. Communication with them was very difficult, as the approach-roads were under fire and there was no telephone-cable except a broken drum or two which had been salvaged from previous occasions. A supporting battery of Field Artillery, however, maintained a forward observation-post near the advanced companies, and messages were sent through it. The gunners were beginning to be short of ammunition.

The Germans attacked heavily about five o'clock, and a report came that they had broken through on the left. The Black Watch had orders to hold the river-bank till nine. They did.

New orders came to hold it for another hour, and this was done. Then it must be denied to the enemy till eleven, and with this last command came instructions to throw everything away but their weapons and the clothes they wore, to make room for all in the ammunition-trucks that were waiting for them. There was rapid destruction of all manner of gear, from tartan trews to wireless transmitters, and then, thinning out from their positions, they marched for some miles, found their transport, and were driven to Ouville.

But they had no rest at Ouville. Before the dawn broke they were ordered to move again and hold a line along the railway that runs through St Pierre-le-Viger. The Division was marching now to the last chapter of its story, and Fate was in a hurry.

Falling Back on St Valéry

To Divisional Headquarters at La Chaussée the early morning of the 10th had brought the news that German tanks were approaching Dieppe from the neighbourhood of Tôtes, which the French were believed to be holding. This report came in at half-past five. An hour later it was confirmed by information that the tanks were then within six miles of La Chaussée. Two-pounder anti-tank guns were ordered to block the road, and at eight o'clock the tanks were temporarily halted after they had advanced another three miles.

This was the altered situation which Major Johnston had to report to the Commander of Ark Force at Le Havre, and within a few hours of his leaving the apparent isolation of the Division had become a certainty. News came that enemy tanks had been seen west of the river Durdent, which empties itself into the Channel some five or six miles beyond St Valéry, and the hope of withdrawing to Le Havre had to be discarded. The General called his Brigadiers into conference: though St Valéry-en-Caux was a poor, unhandy port, the Navy was prepared to do all in its power to evacuate the Allied forces from it, and they must move rapidly to hold and cover the little town. A perimeter was drawn, like a box, about St Valéry, and the dispositions were made.

The proposal to evacuate to St Valéry had reached the Navy at 4 a.m. on June 10th. The Commander-in-Chief himself proceeded to Havre to examine the changed situation. Immediate preparations were made, and destroyers were sent along the coast. They found that the enemy had already mounted guns on the cliffs. The destroyer *Ambuscade* was hit at 3.30 p.m. on June 10th

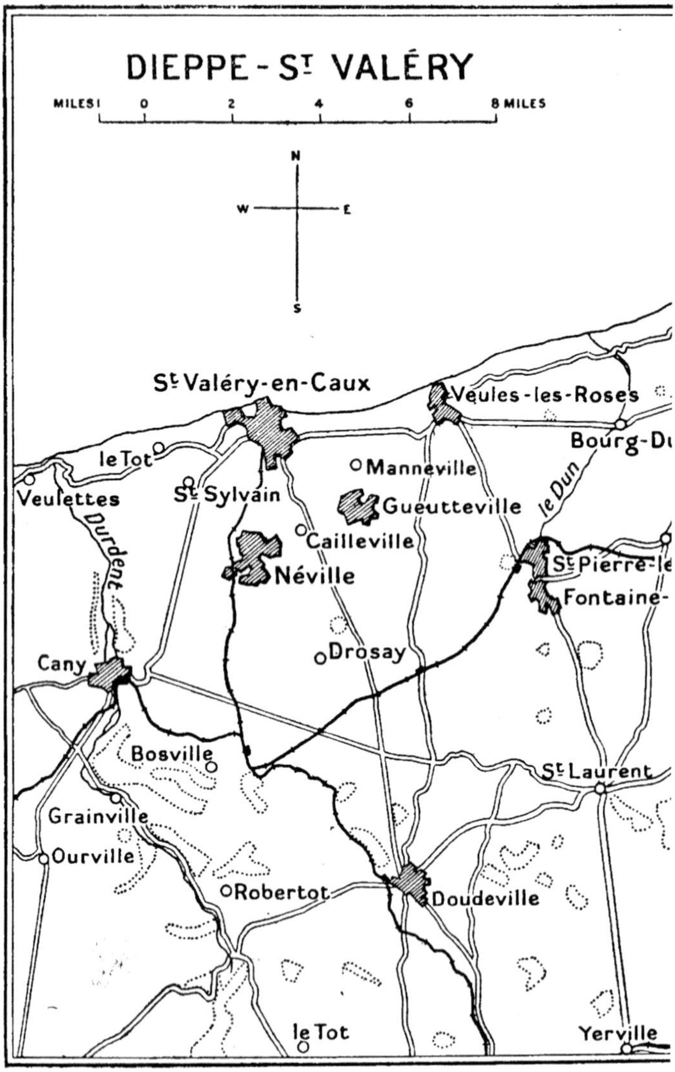
DIEPPE - S^T VALÉRY
MILES 1 0 2 4 6 8 MILES
N
W
E
S
St Valéry-en-Caux
Veules-les-Roses
Bourg-Du
le Tot
Manneville
Veulettes
St Sylvain
Gueutteville
le Dun
Durdent
Cailleville
St Pierre-le
Néville
Fontaine-
Drosay
Cany
Bosville
St Laurent
Grainville
Ourville
Robertot
Doudeville
le Tot
Yerville

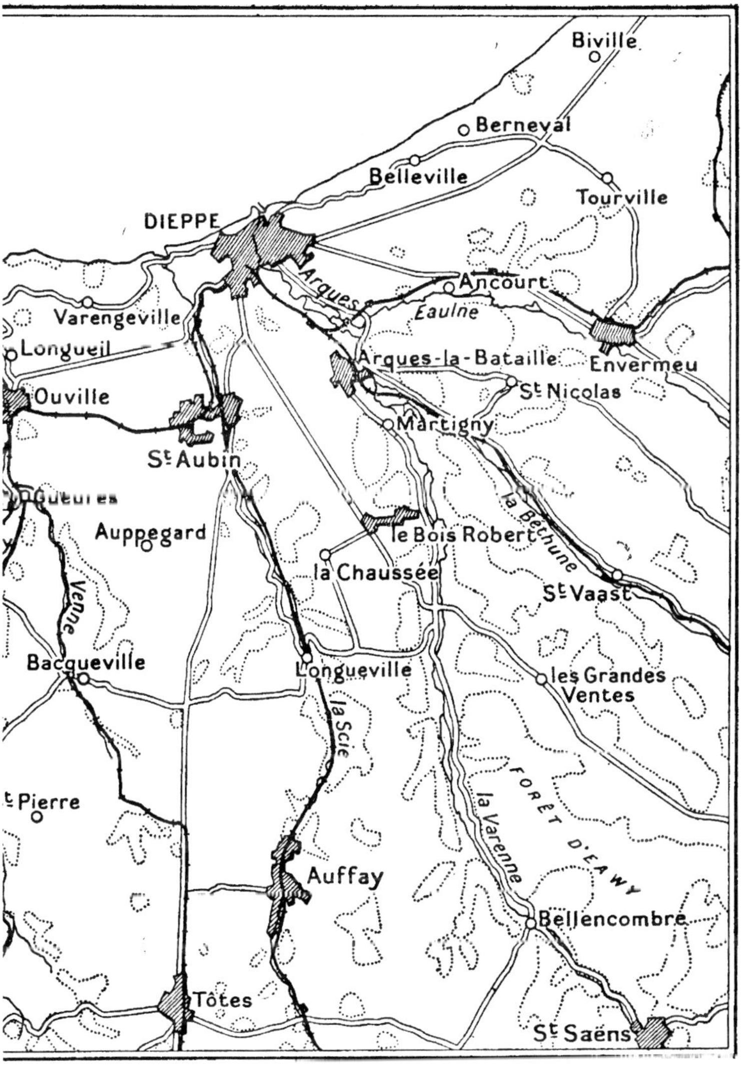

Biville
Berneval
Belleville
Tourville
DIEPPE
Arques
Ancourt
Eaulne
Varengeville
Longueil
Arques-la-Bataille
Envermeu
St Nicolas
Ouville
Martigny
St Aubin
Gueures
la Béthune
Auppegard
le Bois Robert
la Chaussée
St Vaast
Venne
Bacqueville
Longueville
les Grandes Ventes
la Scie
Pierre
FORÊT D'EAWY
la Varenne
Auffay
Bellencombre
Tôtes
St Saëns

while reconnoitring St Valéry, and the destroyer *Boadicea* was heavily engaged at Veulettes at 4.30 some four miles west of St Valéry whilst taking off 60 soldiers. The ships were off St Valéry on the night of the 10th, and boats entered the harbour to bring troops off, but could not find any there, though the rescue tug *Stalwart* took off a number of wounded. Early next day, June 11th, the destroyer *Restigouche* went along to Veulles, four miles to the eastward and took off some troops from the beach. It was understood at the time that the French had not consented to the evacuation, and their consent did not arrive until 5 p.m. on the 11th.

On the general line of the Béthune there had been four battalions forward, and three in rear. The latter—the 2nd Seaforths, the 4th Gordons, and the 1st Gordons—were ordered to establish the western side of the box along the Durdent, the forward battalions would retire and hold a line running southward from Veules-les-Roses to Fontaine-le-Dun, or thereabout. A battalion of the Duke of Wellington's Regiment—a part of Beauman Division, picked up in Dieppe—would form the left flank at Veules, with the 4th Seaforths and the 5th Gordons to south of them, and the 1st Black Watch on the right. These were the sides of the box, and the French, it was intended, would fill the bottom of it. But the French were slow on the road, and until they could take position the Lothians would reconnoitre the gap, and the Norfolks, the Pioneer Battalion, in Divisional reserve, would be prepared to cover it. Even on the Saar the Pioneers had had experience of the fact that their duty always includes fighting as well as pick-and-shovel work; and the Yeomanry, under the indefatigable Colonel Ansell—who had a kind of genius for suddenly appearing in the very place where he was needed—had throughout the brief campaign been busy as a maid-of-all-work, as fiercely mobile as His Majesty's destroyers.

The move was made at night, and despite all efforts by the hard-working Divisional Provost Company to control traffic, the road from Ouville was, in some places, as crowded as the road to Epsom on Derby Day. The French were in retreat, many in total disorder. Not all, indeed, had cast away discipline with hope—before the day was done the Black Watch were to see Frenchmen of a different mettle—but great numbers were in open flight. By good fortune, however, neither Luftwaffe nor German tanks were active in the early hours of the 11th, and by nine o'clock, or earlier, the sides of the box about St Valéry were occupied, and the Highland battalions had begun to dig themselves in.

A Short Left Hook

But the perimeter was never established as a fully defended line. Though there were definite areas of resistance, it was impossible to effect continuity of resistance. There had been no chance to reconnoitre positions, and the Germans were still moving with a devastating speed. They were again exploiting their favourite attack: a left hook, and this time a short left hook. They had not thrust lengthily against Le Havre, but northwards to Dieppe and again to Fécamp. And now the left hook to Fécamp was turning swiftly and snakily to the east.

The Lothians and Border Horse, after shepherding the Allied left along the coast, had retired from Arques to Longueil, where one of the squadrons had some altercation with three stout-hearted Norman farmers who, mistaking them for Germans, opposed the tanks with shot-guns. Now they were ordered to reconnoitre the river Durdent—not, as had been intended, the open bottom of the box, but its western side—and they found the Germans in strong possession of the bridge at Cany, in considerable force near the coastal hamlet of Veulettes; the intervening bridges had been blown.

The squadrons went into action, and though two tanks were lost at Cany, the situation there was stabilised, and a reconnaissance to Bosville, south-east of it, brought news that it was held securely by the French, with no Germans in sight. But on the coast about Veulettes the danger was imminently great. "C" squadron was reinforced and ordered to hold the enemy at all costs, but by eight o'clock at night it was reported to be withdrawing towards St Valéry, and till darkness the German attack was strongly pressed. The other squadrons fell back on Cailleville.

On the eastern perimeter, in the meanwhile, the 4th Seaforths and the 5th Gordons had been fairly heavily engaged, and had suffered casualties. The 1st Black Watch, at St Pierre-le-Viger, were on a forward slope with little cover and their right flank bare. They had no rations till they found some biscuits in a deserted N.A.A.F.I. dump, but they killed a cow and added half-cooked beef to hard tack. At one o'clock an order came to reconnoitre a line from Gueutteville to Cailleville, to which, it was said, they would withdraw in the late afternoon, and be prepared to embark that night.

At ten o'clock General Fortune had issued to his Commanding Officers the following *directives*:

> "The Navy will probably make an effort to take us off by boat, perhaps to-night, perhaps in two nights. I wish all ranks to realise that this can only be achieved by the full co-operation of everyone. Men may have to walk five or six miles. The utmost discipline must prevail.
>
> "Men will board the boats with equipment and carrying arms. Vehicles will be rendered useless without giving away what is being done. Carriers should be retained as the final rearguard. Routes back to the nearest highway should be reconnoitred and officers detailed as guides. Finally, if the enemy should attack before the whole force is evacuated, all ranks must realise that it is up to them to

defeat them. He may attack with tanks, and we have quite a number of anti-tank guns behind. If the infantry can stop the enemy's infantry, that is all that is required, while anti-tank guns and rifles inflict casualties on armoured fighting vehicles."

In the afternoon Fortune received from Colonel Butler, commanding Le Havre garrison, a very dubious confirmation of the arrangements for evacuation. A letter informed him that the Commander-in-Chief at Portsmouth was prepared to send ships to the neighbourhood of St Valéry or to any other place that Fortune might prefer. The Admiral wanted to know the present location of the Fifty-First, its possible location on the following day, Fortune's strength, and his intention. But the letter was brought by a warship whose commander had been instructed to look for the Division at Ouville, ten miles to the east of Fortune's new Headquarters at Cailleville; and the lack of communications which imposed this lack of knowledge—of position and of intention—was a constant reminder of the frailty of plans and projects for joint action.

The Fighting French

The two forward companies of the Black Watch at St Pierre-le-Viger fought stiffly during the late afternoon against ever-increasing German pressure, and by six o'clock some fifty men were wounded or dead. The Commanding Officer, Lieutenant-Colonel Honeyman, had gone back to Brigade Headquarters, and was prevented by machine-gun fire from returning. German tanks appeared at half-past four, and the Signal Officer went to the Battalion's rear Headquarters to bring up the anti-tank platoon. But he, too, was cut off. The Colonel found a way to his other companies, about three-quarters of a mile distant, which at seven o'clock were attacked by numerous tanks. The attack was beaten off, but it was renewed at dawn and the companies were overrun.

The forward companies were latterly commanded by the Adjutant, Captain B. C. Bradford, but senior to Bradford was a French cavalry officer who had arrived in mid-afternoon with a squadron of hard-bitten old soldiers who fought with the utmost gallantry and determination. They picketed their horses in a wood and joined the battle as infantry. When first one flank and then the other was threatened, the French moved briskly to meet the danger, and not the most accurate shell-fire could keep their heads down. Their Commandant, an oldish man, had one arm blown off by a mortar-bomb. His face was grey with approaching death, but two troopers carried him round his position and he repeated his orders: they would hold their line till dark.

13. The Defence of St Valéry

ALL ALONG the eastern perimeter the line was held against a bombardment of infantry-guns and mortars, against tanks that came in behind a curtain of mortar-bombs, and dive-bombers that had no enemy in the sky to hinder them. But though the eastern line stood firm, there were bewildering reports of fighting nearer to St Valéry, and communication with Divisional or Brigade Headquarters became almost impossible because the enemy's machine-gunners were waiting on every road for despatch-riders.

In the town itself there was already more cause for alarm than on the eastern defences: the box had been entered through its western side. The three battalions ordered to hold the Durdent had had no time to reach the river, and Fortune himself had given them an alternative line running southward from the hamlet of Le Tot. The 2nd Seaforths astride the road through Le Tot were in two woods, and a company of the Norfolks was doing its best to fill a wide gap between them and the Camerons. When the German armoured division came in from Veulettes, the Seaforths were in evil plight, for they had left their anti-tank platoon with the Duke of Wellington's on the other side of St Valéry; and so long as the enemy stayed beyond the effective range of anti-tank rifles, they could do little more than show their capacity for taking punishment. But this, of course, was no new experience. Every battalion in the Division had suffered, day after day, from the inadequacy of their weapons. Firing their little two-inch mortars—few enough even of them—against the infantry-guns and innumerable heavy mortars of the enemy, they had all exclaimed, at one time or another, with the same bitterness of frustration, "If only we could get at them!" But wishes make no headway against superior fire-power.

So the Seaforths took their gruel in the woods of Le Tot, and the tanks went through. Not without loss, indeed, for the Highlanders exacted toll of them, and gunners behind the infantry punished them again. But the Germans broke through. They took from the French, and held it, the bluff hill that shelters St Valéry from the Channel winds, and there was close fighting about the south-western outskirts of the town. Throughout the afternoon it had been shelled by guns of small calibre, and bombed at intervals from the air. A good many fires were started, and some French wounded were showing signs of anxiety. But the civil population had either fled or gone to ground in their cellars, and there was no more disorder in the town than the occasional stampede of two or three hundred Army mules which had found precarious freedom in the streets. The only troops in St Valéry, except for a few men of the R.A.S.C. and Divisional Headquarters, were the 51st Anti-Tank Regiment, most of the Norfolks, and a company of the Kensingtons, whose orders were to hold a narrow circle round the outskirts, and cover the final withdrawal of troops from the perimeter.

But the possibility of such a withdrawal was menaced by the appearance, under a heavy smoke-screen, of German tanks and motor-cyclists at the south-west corner of the town; and about five or six o'clock the streets were suddenly filled with the chatter and whine of machine-gun fire. The attack was beaten off, but patrols who went out—signallers from Aberdeen for the most part—found clusters of tanks all round the town, not trying to force an entry, but waiting, sinister and still.

"*Take that to your German General*"

Final arrangements for evacuation had been made at a conference attended by Victor Fortune, the French General commanding the IXth Corps, and officers of the Royal Navy; and beaches had been allotted to French and British. Embarkation was to begin at half-past ten, and orders were sent round the perimeter that when everything had been destroyed except the arms and ammunition a man could carry, the troops were to withdraw into the town. These orders, however, failed to reach the 2nd Seaforths, who remained in the woods.

At half-past nine Major Rennie, G.S.O. II, and a naval officer reconnoitred the beaches, and both in the town and on the promenade were fired on by machine-guns from the west hill. Earlier in the day the naval officer had been surprised by the German tank attack, and nearly captured. He had arrived in St Valéry with a new code-book, and this, under machine-gun fire, he managed to burn behind a pile of stones. Now, on the beach, he was waiting for a signal from the relieving ships. He waited till about half-past ten, and no signal came. He and Rennie were rather worried.

From St Pierre-le-Viger, Bradford had sent off as many of his wounded as he could pack into his office-truck and a Bren-carrier. They drove across the fields towards St Valéry. The two diminished companies then held their ground till nearly ten o'clock, when with the French they retired to what was to have been their inner line, between Gueutteville and Cailleville. They reached Gueutteville at half-past one in the morning, but no one there knew anything about the 153rd Brigade. The men were dead-beat and could go no farther, so they slept for two hours on the stone floor of a schoolhouse.

About midnight the Lothians and Border Horse, retiring to Cailleville and thence to St Valéry, could see from four miles away their destination marked by two great pillars of red smoke rising far into the sky. They had destroyed their vehicles, and in accordance with the General's *directives* were prepared to embark.

The entrance to the town is a narrow way between bluff heights and the men were told they must go quietly and in single file, as the Germans were on both sides. They had orders to make for the station, but there they could find no one to give them further instructions. There were soldiers of all kinds in the narrow twisting streets, and most of the houses were on fire. Chimney-pots came tumbling down, and smouldering beams crashed in a shower of sparks. At intervals a star-shell rose and fell with a white glare upon the crowded, smoking alleys. The harbour was difficult to find, and when they reached it there were no ships there.

In fact naval ships had been waiting off the coast since the afternoon of the 10th, and, as already described, had entered St Valéry on the night of the 10th, leaving in the morning. The transports and boats had then assembled north of the harbour before midday on the 11th. They were heavily bombed by aircraft and subjected to accurate fire from batteries on the cliffs, so that orders had to be issued then to move farther off the coast. Later on June 11th the evacuation commenced at Havre and orders to evacuate at St Valéry came from the Admiralty at the same time, but it was then too late. Fog had come down, delaying the return of the ships and obscuring from view all the coast. The tug *Fair Play* closed the beach about 12.30 a.m. on June 12th, slightly west of St Valéry, and landed beach parties. Heavy fire was opened on them at once and four boats were sunk. The cliffs and the town were securely occupied by the enemy. The destroyer *Codrington* proceeded to Veulles, escorting some eight vessels. She landed beach parties and began to take men off successfully in spite of heavy machine-gun fire. The sloop *Hebe II* took off 80 soldiers from the beach close to St Valéry, but she was sunk and lost with her commanding officer. On shore it was reported that a naval tow of four or five boats, trying to enter, had been sunk by gun-fire, and no other ships had come in. The latest news was that no ships were coming.

It had begun to rain. The news was confirmed that there would be no evacuation that night. The patient soldiers, packed tightly in the darkness, took this newest blow, this fearful disappointment, with stoic fortitude. They did not grumble, and if they felt despair they hid it under calm acceptance. They obeyed their orders, and moving into the eastward part of the town, prepared to defend themselves within a small perimeter for another day. There was still some hope—or perhaps only the fiction of a hope—that the Navy would come for them. But stronger than hope was discipline. Discipline was unimpaired.

At half-past three in the morning the Germans sent an envoy to the Seaforths in the woods around Le Tot. He arrived in a tank, carrying a white flag, and brought false tidings; there had been a general surrender, he said, of the French IXth Corps and the 51st Division. He requested the Seaforths to follow suit.

The Seaforths, uncertain whether to believe him but

certainly unwilling to submit, asked for time to consider the demand. They had in the woods a large number of wounded men, who badly needed medical attention. It might be possible, they thought, to get their wounded cared for and mislead the enemy as well. Volunteers were called for. A considerable party of men emerged from the woods and walked—or limped or were carried—into the German lines. The enemy, apparently, believed that the Seaforths had surrendered. But their prisoners were only the wounded and the men who had volunteered to attend them. The remainder of the battalion, and all surviving officers, lay hidden in the wood till darkness came again. Then, dividing into little parties, they scattered and tried to break through the German ring. But very few had any luck, and only a handful finally escaped.

Elsewhere, and nearer to St Valéry, another demand for surrender had been more flatly rejected by an officer of the 1st Gordons. Second-Lieutenant P. B. Hay, in charge of his Battalion's transport, had spent much of the day on shell-swept roads, striving with dogged valiance to maintain communication between his Headquarters and the transport echelon. Cut off at last by increased shelling and the ever-tightening congestion of traffic, he brought his command to the outskirts of St Valéry—some hamlet on the edge of it, or suburban colony—and found confusion there. The road was blocked. Two big French lorries, overturned, were burning fiercely. There were soldiers there who had lost their units, stragglers, men without leaders. Hay took command of the situation.

With great energy and initiative he organised local defence. He gathered the lost men, formed sections and platoons, established them in defensive positions. His authority was recognised, and when a French officer, some poor renegade, came with a message from the enemy, it was Hay to whom he was taken, and from whom he got his answer. It was brief, it was loud, it was impolite. "Take that to your German General," said Hay.

Later, when shelling intensified, Hay withdrew his positions, and till late at night maintained his command intact. When he was last seen he was going his rounds, maintaining order where it was threatened, creating order where there was confusion.

Private McCready Writes Home

Private McCready, who has been quoted before, makes a vivid picture of the chaos that by now existed in parts of the surrounding countryside. He and some others had got lost the night before, because a truck-driver fell asleep, and after escaping from enemy country they reached Brigade Headquarters by devious routes.

"All the main roads," he says, "were simply choked with French troops on foot, and refugees, occasionally we passed piles of them dead at the roadside, having been machine-gunned from the air or just rolled aside by tanks. How we ever got out of that was a miracle. We never got back to the Battalion after that. We were stuck in an orchard near Brigade and we just simply waited for things to happen. Mr. Telfer-Smollett went off to reconnoitre new positions about mid-day, and never returned.

"By this time we were being shelled, machine-gunned, and I think all the weapons that could be used were against us, this continued until after dark, and I am afraid I fell asleep at the roadside. Mr. Allison gave out all the cigarettes he had and we just simply lay there. At two o'clock in the morning"—the morning of the 12th, that is—"I was told it was a case of every man for himself, so we all got bundled into the remaining five trucks and I must say I was completely unaware of what direction the coast lay in, or what was to be done, in fact, I was beyond caring about anything.

"Well, we moved off. I was in the back of the 8 cwt. with somebody sitting on my head. We had only gone half a mile when we were ambushed, by machine-gun. I scrambled out somehow and dived into the ditch, then the enemy started using Very lights and picked the men off with tommy-guns as they jumped off the truck. I owe my life to the fact that I was in the last truck. I managed to scramble out of the ditch and along the bank. I almost got a burst into my back. They were using tracer and they almost burnt my ears with the heat. I came on a party of R.E's at the roadside and they immediately scattered into the fields. I saw Mr. Allison there, he was all right, he followed some R.E's who went off to the right.

"I waited a few minutes, and then made off after the ones who went to the left. We were spotted in the light and murderous fire broke out again, I don't know how far I crawled on my stomach, it seemed hours before that gunner got fed up, so with his last burst we gave him a volley from our rifles and it evidently disposed of him as the going was comparatively easy for a bit, until we ran into an enemy motor-convoy on the road. It was stopped, and I thought it was French. They must have got a surprise because we were well away when they opened fire on us. I don't think they hit anybody as it was fairly misty and that coupled with the darkness helped us. After that it was fairly easy to the cliffs."

The Black Watch See it Through

At a quarter to four the Black Watch roused in their schoolhouse and continued their march to St Valéry. During the night it had begun to rain, and now it was raining hard. After a mile or two they were halted by an almost impassable mass of deserted transport. Bradford found a bicycle and made his way to Cailleville to look for the rest of the Battalion. But Cailleville was deserted. He collected two waterproofs and a tin of chocolate biscuits from deserted staff cars, and was about to return to his companies when he discovered that someone had stolen his bicycle. He found another, and presently met Major Dundas, second-in-command of the Battalion, who told him that the order to hold the Cailleville line had been cancelled. Dundas had forty men, Bradford a hundred. They found a ration dump, and issued bully-beef and biscuits.

At a quarter to eight they encountered a Brigade Major who told them to take up a position on high ground near a cemetery about a mile and a half north-east of St Valéry—on the ground that Fortune had chosen for his last stand, that is. The command was organised, and a search of the hundreds of deserted trucks that littered the nearby roads produced Bren guns, anti-tank rifles, ammunition and rations. Stragglers were collected and armed. The rump of the Black Watch, well-found and fed, were again ready for action, and had not long to wait for it. Presently they were being mortared from front and rear, and tanks came in upon their left flank. They could see some French officers with white cloths pinned to their backs, but thought only that this must be some eccentric form of identification. It was still raining.

Elsewhere on the eastern skirts of St Valéry, Camerons, Gordons and Seaforths, with discipline and native resolution to combat mortal weariness, had in like manner organised their last resistance. But confusion by now was more typical of the scene than order, and discipline prevailed as islands in a fearful chaos. The white clouts on the French officers' shoulders were more significant than the Black Watch had thought. The French had already surrendered. At some time during the night of the 11th a French artillery regiment had told the Kensingtons that the war was over, and at eight o'clock on the morning of the 12th our Allies capitulated.

The Braver Choice

There was indeed no reason, save honour, for fighting any longer. The Germans were in St Valéry. They had established their light field-pieces, their heavy mortars and machine-guns, about the harbour and in commanding positions overlooking the port. The Navy could not enter. Through the rain over the Channel no one could see the promise of a White Ensign. The hope of escape had vanished.

But Victor Fortune had still to make his decision, and it was not easy. The hard core of the Fifty-First was fighting still, and would fight till its last platoon was overwhelmed. Was it possible to organise a counter-attack on the German positions about the harbour, and still maintain outward defence against the day's new pressure from east and west and south? Was there any hope, any chance at all, of regaining the town and holding it for another night?

The men were weary to the very bone. Since the first week of May they had had no proper rest. There had been no chance to refurbish and reorganise the battalions after their fighting on the Saar. There had come instead the long march across France, and then the hurried advance to the Somme and the days of fighting before Abbeville. Then the contested retreat, with rearguard action by day and the dive-bombers screaming from the sun, and by night the forced marches over roads that were a nightmare of lost souls and bewildered traffic. His Highlanders and their English companions in arms had left their dead in every Norman field from the Somme to the little Durdent, from the Cambron woods to the trees about the cemetery where the Black Watch were now at bay. Only a fragment of the Division remained, and those who survived were at the last pitch of their endurance.

There was yet a stronger argument than human exhaustion.

Not a round remained of gun ammunition; the Royal Artillery, which had fought throughout the retreat with dexterous gallantry and great accomplishment, had fired their last shells before they took the breech-blocks from their guns and left them to the enemy. The Sappers had no stores: they had long been fighting as infantry, and on the Bresle a Field Company—the 26th—had been seen conducting itself with as much aptitude for battle as if it had been born, bred, taught and trained to be nothing else than infantry. But even the hardiest of infantry soldiers need more than a rifle and a clip of cartridges, and to lighten the load that was to have been embarked, Fortune had given orders that all stores and vehicles and equipment should be destroyed, all gear cast away except what weapons a man could carry. But the Germans had their artillery, their abundance of mortars, their machine-guns. To order a few companies of exhausted riflemen, with Bren guns in support, to attack such a weight of metal would be little better than homicide. But the alternative was surrender, and the burden of such an act would rest on him. . . .

Fortune never shrank from making a decision. Now, facing the hardest question of all, he took the braver choice.

At ten o'clock Major Thomas Rennie went to the cemetery hill and gave the remnant of the Black Watch their orders. They were to cease fire and surrender.

No one believed him, because the order, at first hearing, was unbelievable. But Rennie was well known, and his word could not long be doubted. With understanding came utter dismay, and men stood up and wept. A furlong distant the mortar detachment continued to fight against a troop of tanks. Not until they had been individually commanded to surrender did they cease fire.

A little while later the last fragment of the Gordon Highlanders, unarmed, were allowed to march past their General. Marching in the rain, they gave him *Eyes right!* And the Fifty-First Division went into eclipse.

14. "Scorched Earth" and Escape

EAST OF St Valéry there are cliffs, three hundred feet high, reaching without a break to the little port of Veules-les-Roses, four miles away. When the Navy on the night of June 11th discovered that it was impossible to evacuate troops from St Valéry, they proceeded to Veulles-les-Roses four miles to the eastward, landed beach parties and began evacuating the troops found there. In spite of machine-gun fire from the cliffs they succeeded in taking off about 1,350 British and 930 French soldiers. These were the little groups of men, more fortunate than many others, who responded to *sauve qui peut* by heading eastward. They had had a perilous route to travel. Major C. J. Y. Dallmeyer, of the Lothians and Border Horse, who successfully led a party from St Valéry to the cliffs, saw, when daylight came, the dim shape of vessels lying offshore, and knew there was a break in the cliff at Veules. When he got there he found five gullies leading to the beach, of which three were allotted to French troops and two to British. They formed a queue and waited their turn. German aeroplanes flew over, but did no damage. Small boats were coming ashore and ferrying-off their passengers. Presently they were taken aboard a ship, which already was being shelled from St Valéry.

On his way to Veules, Dallmeyer had seen a large number of men going down the cliff on improvised ropes, but, not unwisely, had decided against so uncertain a route. Private McCready, however, risked his neck and brought it safely home:

"There was no way down the cliffs which were three hundred feet high, and a sheer drop. Someone started making a rope of rifle-slings, and I joined in, by the time we had it made it was daylight, and the enemy were shelling from both sides. I was fourth man on the rope and it was two and a half hours before I got down. The first man to go met his death as the slings snapped, but it was either chance it or get caught so over I went, what a drop; and bullets spattering all over. We were being machine-gunned and sniped, all the time. However, I got down without mishap, and struggled along two miles of beach to the boats.

"What a lot of dead men on that beach—it was littered with them. I had just got into the small boat when the bombers came, one boat was sunk with about thirty men in it, only one man was saved. The ships put up a terrific barrage and brought down two planes. How I got on the ship is still a bit of a dream to me, but get on I did, and soaked to the skin and simply covered with mud. I just sprawled out on deck, out for the count, I soon got a rude awakening, the enemy started shelling from the cliff tops, but the destroyers put paid to their career. All those who had rifles had to get up on the top deck and fire at the planes. So I fired my remaining bandolier.

"We lay there until it was decided that no more men could possibly be on the beach or on the cliffs."

That was about ten o'clock on the morning of the 12th.

Havre—A Knacker's Yard

The same hour was spent by Ark Force in making of Le Havre a knacker's yard. Hundreds of motor vehicles were being smashed, initially by driving one against another so as to crumple bonnet and stern, then with hammer, crowbar, or heavy spanner. Petrol stores and oil refineries had been set on fire the day before. . . .

Three days earlier the C.R.A. had ordered the 51st Medium Regiment of Royal Artillery to move at once from its sites in the Bois Robert and try to cross the Seine at Rouen. The regiment had no information about the German positions, nor of Allied troops in the area. It had to travel, with eleven guns and a hundred and ten vehicles, across the front of the advancing German columns for a distance of nearly thirty miles.

Two parallel roads crossed the debatable flank, and both were reconnoitred. One patrol returned. The route was decided and a rendezvous appointed south of the Seine. The Commanding Officer, with his Adjutant, his Regimental Sergeant-Major and four despatch-riders, led the way. They arrived in Rouen at ten a.m. and found an array of oil-tanks burning into a huge black cloud. One road-bridge still crossed the river, but when they were two hundred yards from it, it was blown up. The suspension bridge was also blown, and Germany's Fifth Column began sniping from houses in the vicinity. French columns of considerable size were trying to cross the river by any means that remained, and the Colonel decided that his regiment would stand no chance against such competition. He ordered it to a wood three miles out of Rouen, and the Adjutant went to reconnoitre Pont de l'Arche, ten miles to the south-east.

The Colonel went to look at a ferry eight or nine miles to the west, but the only road to it was impenetrably blocked by French transport and refugees. He decided to go to Le Havre, and found on the way that the intervening ferries had been stopped by order of the French military authorities, and roads leading to them were closed.

A similar attempt to save stores and heavy transport had been made by the 154th Brigade Signals and Light

Aid Detachment, moving east from Le Havre. They set out with machine-guns in the leading vehicles, a four-gallon tin of petrol in each, and the men were instructed that if they were ambushed they were to puncture the tins, set the transport on fire, and return to Le Havre on foot if they could. The column consisted of about eighty vehicles. Not a boat was to be seen on the north bank of the Seine, and the road was littered with civilian cars, broken-down or abandoned. They arrived at Lillebonne and found it in ruins, burning fiercely in one vast fire that was fed by an oil refinery which French Sappers had destroyed.

French sentries guarded the Quillebeuf ferry. Nearly thirty vehicles got safely across, then the sound of firing was heard in Lillebonne, and the ferry did not return. The remainder of the column had to go back to Le Havre.

The 154th Brigade Gets Away

At nine o'clock on the 11th Brigadier Stanley–Clarke gave orders that the Gonserville–Montivilliers–Octeville line must be held to the last round and the last man. He knew then that the remaining Brigades of the Fifty-First were in desperate plight. He knew that Fortune meant to keep step with the French 31st Division, which could march only eighteen kilometres a day, and he knew that before they could arrive he would have to fight to keep the port open. But he was still hopeful that Fortune and his tattered battalions would get through.

Then the Navy reported that the other Brigades were completely cut off, and an attempt would be made to embark them a: St Valéry. Thereupon arrangements were immediately made for the evacuation of Ark Force and the garrison of Le Havre. Embarkation would begin that night, and the naval authorities insisted that, once it had begun, it must be continuous. The Luftwaffe had been very active over Le Havre—three transports, lying outside the harbour, had been sunk on the 10th, and a transit camp intensively bombed—but the Royal Air Force had arranged to give support on the 12th.

"A" Brigade was withdrawn from the Lillebonne–Bréaute positions and safely embarked during the night of the 11th along with all troops but those manning the inner line. The rain gave some protection against German aircraft, and only a few bombs were dropped.

It had been arranged that the inner line should be evacuated at noon on the 12th, but in the morning the French Command very earnestly requested that it be held for another twelve hours to enable scattered elements of their IXth Corps to reach Le Havre. This was conceded, and the afternoon was spent in salvaging tools from the columns of ruined transport, and completing their destruction. A subaltern of the 17th Field Regiment, enterprising and knowledgeable about shipping, got seventeen of his regiment's 25 pounders embarked and safely to Cherbourg. Then the knacker's yard sprouted fires and explosions, and the enemy's reconnaissance planes, impressed by the dismal enormity of destruction, presumably reported that all troops had left the town. The Luftwaffe left it alone that night, and the last of the 154th Brigade was evacuated without difficulty in the early hours of June 13th and landed in Cherbourg.

15. The Auld Alliance

THE TWO ferry loads of heavy vehicles which had been successful in crossing the river at Quillebeuf made slow progress by congested road to Le Mans, and there the drivers found fellow-countrymen: the forward elements of the Fifty-Second, the Lowland Division.

As if to symbolise the phœnix quality of the Auld Alliance—stubbornly renewing itself out of seeming extinction—the regiments of Lowland Scotland came marching into France as the bitter remnant of the Highland battalions went forth from it. Seaforths and Camerons, Gordons and the Black Watch and the Argyll and Sutherland Highlanders had fought to the conclusion of their luck; and now, to try theirs, the Royal Scots and the Highland Light Infantry, Cameronians, and Royal Scots Fusiliers and the King's Own Scottish Borderers were coming in.

A brigade went into action near Faverolles, but their service was short. Paris capitulated, and the Auld Alliance was abrogated by the Government of France.

By the Government, but not by the people. When the captive-column of the Fifty-First had a little recovered from the exhaustion of the first few days—when men marched as if in a fearful dream of weariness and starvation—then some of the stronger and more daring found opportunity to elude their guards and go to cover in a roadside wood. Every day a few more escaped from the long column, and waiting for the night would turn on their tracks and begin a tedious long march to the coast, or farther still to the Spanish frontier. Then it was that the people of France showed their courage and abiding friendship, for in lonely farms or in villages under the very nose of the German conqueror these desperate fugitives found sustenance and willing help.

Some of them went first to familiar places where they had been billeted in the early months of their service, where they had been welcome guests and their pipers so often had gathered a crowd to *Miss Drummond of Perth* and *The Barren Rocks of Aden*. They had roused all northern France to their tunes, and when they marched into Lorraine, into warmer country, into villages that smelt of fruit-blossom—but more strongly of the midden—they would see in the darkness of the night, in the shadow of a house, the glow of cigarettes, and voices would cry hoarsely, "Musique! Jouez le musique!" Then the pipers would play, and the villagers would march alongside the column, friendly and excited.

They had been made welcome to France, and the welcome had been sincere. In the streets of a dozen occupied towns, in Paris itself, in hamlet and farm the sincerity was proved when the men who had escaped from their captors came to ask for help, and were given it by brave and generous hands.

The Hard Core of Discipline

And as many of the people of France put their Government to shame, so did much of its Army repudiate the defeatism of the Grand Quartier-Général. A great mass of soldiers, disillusioned and bewildered, was utterly broken; but many units fought with the spirit and tenacity that once gave Verdun a name in history. De Gaulle's Armoured Division in the battle before Abbeville; the sturdy gunners and drivers of the tanks that led the way up the deadly ridge at Cambron; the Basques, tough and resolute, on the river Bresle; the grim, undaunted cavalry soldiers at St Pierre-le-Viger, the old Commandant with his arm lopped off—men like these are to be remembered, as well as those stricken by the malady of defeat.

But it is, on the whole, against a background of rout and the sickness of despair that the performance of the Fifty-First must be assessed, and the fact that signally emerges is that throughout its rearguard action and retreat the Division retained coherence. It remained a Division, and discipline ruled until the very end. It had shown, both on the Saar and on the Somme, a finely aggressive spirit and great stubbornness in defence. It had discovered a remarkable unwillingness—incapacity is perhaps the better word—to admit defeat, though the odds against it were always heavy. Striking westward towards St Valéry had been the 4th German Corps of two divisions forward, two in reserve; and in the left hook over the Durdent were a Panzer Division and a motorised division behind. But against this impressive strength the Highland officers, non-commissioned officers and private soldiers—and the many Englishmen who enlarged the Division—had revealed, again and again, their sense of responsibility and their gift of initiative. They were compelled to show an almost superhuman endurance.

These are soldierly qualities, and they provide the substance for many heartening paragraphs in a history of misfortune. But what conclusively proves that the Division was a good Division, in spite of misfortune, is its continuing discipline. There is no sterner test of discipline than a long rearguard action, unless it be the sight of supporting troops who have been broken in the fight. The Fifty-First survived those tests, and the Division was a Division till the end. It had no luck—the dice were loaded outrageously against it—and so it failed to maintain the legend that its predecessor had made in the first German war, for a legend needs a little luck to help it grow. But the Fifty-First had the other virtues of the old Division, and the proof is this—that would prove the virtue of any division—that in spite of its accumulated weariness, the frustration of all its hope, the failure on its flank and its grievous losses, its spirit was unbroken. It suffered many casualties, but not the fatal one. Its hard core was fighting to the end, and discipline was last in the field.

THE ARMY AT WAR

Other booklets in this series are:—

THE BATTLE OF FLANDERS
THE NORTHERN GARRISONS
DESTRUCTION OF AN ARMY
THE DEFENCE OF CALAIS
THEY SOUGHT OUT ROMMEL

To be published shortly:—

THE ABYSSINIAN CAMPAIGNS

All the volumes of this series are being reprinted by MLRS due to their significance as records of British military operations.

Please check for updates at www.mlrsbooks.com

MLRS